For all the children I've had the privilege to work with.

You have been my teachers.

Be Their Hero: An Educator's Guide to Trauma-Informed Care
Copyright © 2023 Josh Varner

All rights reserved. No part of this publication may be reproduced, distributed, or transmitted in any form or by any means, including photocopying, recording, or other electronic or mechanical methods, without the prior written permission of the publisher, except in the case of brief quotations embodied in reviews and certain other noncommercial uses permitted by copyright law.

ISBN: 9798851914621

www.joshvarnerconsulting.com
Twitter: @JoshVarner65
Facebook: @josh.varner1

Be Their Hero:

An Educator's Guide to Trauma-Informed Care

By Josh Varner

Introduction

My "Why" *7*

Journey to Becoming a Trauma-Informed Advocate *8*

Table of Contents

Chapter 1: Hero Spotlights & The Kid Who Changed Everything *13*

Chapter 2: The ACE Study, An Overview *19*

Chapter 3: Emotional Dysregulation, "Creative" Coping, & Cognitive Impacts *25*

Chapter 4: What is Trauma & How Does Trauma Wound? *35*

Chapter 5: Trauma's Impact on Educational Outcomes *45*

Chapter 6: This is Your Brain on Trauma *53*

Chapter 7: Fight, Flight, & Freeze in a School Setting *67*

Chapter 8: Triggers *75*

Chapter 9: Three Types of Stress & the Body's Response *87*

Chapter 10: Stuck On, Stuck Off *95*

Chapter 11: Neuroplasticity & the Power of Therapeutic Moments *103*

Chapter 12: Counseling & Trauma-Informed Therapy *115*

Chapter 13: Understanding Attachment *123*

Chapter 14: Social Emotional Skills...129

Chapter 15: Distressed Students & the 3 R's...139

Chapter 16: Self-Regulation & Personal Reflection.......................................151

Chapter 17: Building Relationships: Quality or Quantity?..........................157

Chapter 18: Student Support Plans..167

Chapter 19: Classroom Tools..175

Chapter 20: Trauma Separates Us, A Summary...189

Chapter 21: Ideological Warning & Teacher Self-Care.................................197

Chapter 22: Johnny's Story, Continued...209

Resources & References..213

My "Why"

I've undertaken the task of writing this book because, after training audiences all over the country, I've consistently been asked for more materials they could take home. This book is that material. It is designed to help educators implement practical strategies that support students impacted by childhood trauma. In order to make the information easier to understand and implement, I've taken some liberties to simplify the neuroscience. While there are many others who may explain the neuroscience more accurately and in greater detail, many educators, parents, and students find this information difficult to comprehend or unnecessary to their goal of practical application. It's my hope that by simplifying the conversation, more educators will buy into this movement and use evidence-based tools to support these vulnerable children.

My Journey to Becoming a Trauma-Informed Advocate

While today I speak regularly around the country about trauma-informed education practices, the journey to this point has been a winding one. It began in college where I obtained my Masters Degree in School Counseling in 2003 from the University of Wisconsin-Platteville. Rather than utilizing that degree right away, I spent the next ten years coaching college football. After marrying my wife Ashley and starting a family I decided that I wanted to pursue a career that would allow me to spend more time with them.

The first job I took was as a community-based mental health professional working with children with significant mental health issues. Classes I had taken in college, such as advanced developmental psychology and advanced abnormal psychology did a great job of teaching me how to use the DSM-IV TR for mental health diagnosis. I could meet a young person, look at their symptoms, and label them with a mental health diagnosis. However, the longer I worked in this field, the more I realized these labels did not capture the experiences of these young people as holistically as I felt they should. More importantly, these labels occasionally had a negative impact on how these families and communities viewed them and, most importantly, how these children viewed themselves.

The typical focus following these diagnoses was to manage symptoms rather than attending to root issues, which wasn't very impactful. I found myself frustrated with negative outcomes and feeling burnt out with the profession. I had left a career in coaching where I was vibrant and successful but now, I felt like I wasn't making an impact and was ineffective with my interventions. Thankfully, within a couple of years, I heard my first trauma-informed speaker. That changed everything.

To say that speaker shifted the course of my career would be a significant understatement. Following what I heard that day, I changed course in my life and in my journey working in mental health. Instead of saying, "What's wrong with these kids?" I started focusing on what they had been through. The impact of trauma on later diagnoses and behaviors was undeniable.

Since that training years ago, I have become increasingly focused on and fascinated by the approach of trauma-informed care, particularly for educators. I've read books, listened to podcasts, and attended conferences. Once I understood the power of "therapeutic moments" for rewiring students' brains I knew that in order to make the biggest impact on young people, I needed to see them more than once a week or a few times a month. I also realized that meant our school systems provided the perfect environment to help students recover from trauma, particularly if we could sell educators on being intentional about these interventions eight hours a day for thirteen years. It was at this point that I transitioned to the school system to see this in action for myself.

The years I spent in the school system solidified what I suspected was the essential need for trauma-informed education and educators. The trauma-informed care I saw first-hand was incredibly impactful on students' lives and outcomes. Given that you know what I do now, it's not hard to see where I'm going. Rather than staying in the schools, I felt compelled to get this message out to my community. After so many years in community mental health, as a school counselor, as an at-risk teacher and as a school-based mental health professional, as a speaker, I was now finally spreading a message that could have the ripple effect I was hoping for.

In the pages that follow, you will see how the different roles I've had helped me grow professionally. You will hear about successes and failures as I've tried to implement this important work both on my own and when I've tried to share it with others. Most importantly, you will hear about the direct interventions that I felt were the most impactful in working with students so that you may use them yourselves. Thank you for journeying with me.

Chapter One

Hero Spotlights & The Kid Who Changed Everything

"Trauma is a fact of life. It does not, however, have to be a life sentence. Not only can trauma be healed, but with appropriate guidance and support, it can be transformative." ~ Peter A. Levine

Throughout this book, you will encounter several "Hero Spotlights." For our purposes, a hero is defined as someone who makes a life-altering impact on another person. These stories are provided to inspire you and give you an opportunity to see yourself in some of these amazing people.

In addition to Hero Spotlights, you will learn about several students I've worked with throughout the years. We will also consistently follow a special student named Johnny as his story weaves back and forth between his real life, relevant research, data, and the impacts of childhood trauma.

Meet Johnny

Johnny was a kindergartener when I first met him. On his first day of school, Johnny arrived in dirty clothes, his hair was disheveled, and he was very unkempt. He struggled with following simple rules and directions. At lunch, he didn't know how to use a fork or spoon because he never used one at home. And, educationally, he had no idea what these ABCs or 123s were. Johnny's teacher reached out to his mother several times to try to talk about his needs but was never able to reach her or get a call back. Eventually, the school made a hotline call and the Children's Division arrived at Johnny's home. The home was in disarray and Johnny's Mom was battling a severe methamphetamine addiction. At this time, Johnny was removed from the home and placed into foster care. I was assigned as his community-based mental health provider.

My first impression was that Johnny was a cute little boy, full of energy with very little impulse control. Johnny was unable to relax even for a moment. His eyes would dart around the room and it seemed he didn't have anyone to trust. During this time, we were very fortunate to find a kinship placement for him. Even though she had almost no relationship with him prior to the removal, Johnny was placed with his Grandma, who turned out to be his first hero.

Ironically, Johnny's Grandma had just retired that week and intended to travel the country in an RV with her boyfriend. Instead, she put her life on hold and took him in. And while Grandma met his physical needs with healthy food, a safe home, clean clothes, and proper hygiene, that didn't make Johnny's emotional struggles go away. As just a short list of challenges, Johnny would tear apart his room and run away from her home. Despite how exhausting it was, Grandma was a rock through all the storms and kept meeting the needs of her grandson.

In addition to challenges in his new home, Johnny also struggled at first in his new school. Fortunately, Johnny found two more heroes there. Johnny's kindergarten teacher was amazing. She was one of those masterful snake charmers of a teacher who seemed to effortlessly get children to line up and follow directions. Her classroom was very trauma-informed friendly, safe and predictable with an established routine. Over time, this allowed Johnny to be able to predict what was going to happen next and he began to feel safe with her and in her classroom.

Johnny's second school hero was his school counselor. They worked together almost every day, building a loving and trusting relationship while developing coping strategies, impulse control, and social skills. Johnny's counselor helped him learn to engage his peers appropriately and how to resolve conflict with them. The impact of these heroes was beginning to compound in Johnny's life.

As Johnny's community-based mental health professional, it was my job to work with him on his social-emotional skills. It was also my job to help the team collaborate together to make sure we were providing Johnny consistent care at work, home, and in the community. While this took time, we slowly made progress. Johnny's behaviors at home and school got a little better each day. Incrementally, we saw less of his negative behaviors and more positive ones. Through the impact of these heroes, Johnny's path was finally headed in a positive direction. Throughout this book, we will continue to follow Johnny's story, learn how his traumatic past impacted his daily life, and additional challenges these heroes faced trying to support this amazing child.

Reflection Questions

1. What experiences in your journey brought you to a career in education?

2. Do you have a "Johnny"? How has that impacted your work?

Chapter Two

The ACE Study, An Overview

Unlike simple stress, trauma changes your view of your life and yourself. It shatters your most basic assumptions about yourself and your world — "Life is good," "I'm safe," "People are kind," "I can trust others," "The future is likely to be good" — and replaces them with feelings like "The world is dangerous," "I can't win," "I can't trust other people," or "There's no hope."
~ *Mark Goulston MD*

While we will discuss many real-life examples throughout this book, it is also important to consider the valuable research and data that inform the trauma-informed care movement. One of the most important is ACE, which stands for Adverse Childhood Experience. Conducted in the late 1990s by the Center for Disease Control (CDC) and Kaiser Permanente, the ACE study is the largest-ever study of childhood trauma. The stunning results made it a landmark study in the trauma-informed care movement and it remains relevant and regularly cited and utilized today. And, while I could write an entire book on this essential research, I'm going to consolidate the critical information into one chapter to highlight the main points.

The sample of this study was enormous, with over 17,000 people taking the ACE questionnaire. The information they gave was then compared to their current health and behaviors. As a method of measurement, participants in the study were given an ACE score depending on the number of challenging life experiences they had before the age of 18. The experiences included were: emotional abuse, physical abuse, sexual abuse, mother treated violently, substance abuse in the home, mental illness in the home, parent separation, incarcerated household member, emotional neglect, and physical neglect. If a participant lived through 5 of these challenges they would have an ACE score of 5, if they suffered through all 10 they would have an ACE score of 10, and if they didn't encounter any of them they would have an ACE score of zero. From this, researchers wanted to study whether an individual's ACE score correlated with future health outcomes and behaviors.

Overall, researchers found that ACES are very common, with nearly ⅔ of the study's participants having at least one ACE, one out of five people with three or more ACES, and one out of eight with four or more ACEs.

In addition to identifying ACEs as common experiences, the researchers were able to connect the number of childhood ACEs with adverse adult outcomes. People with an ACE score of six or more died, on average, twenty years earlier than those who had zero. Five out of the six leading causes of death in the United States double once someone gets to four or more ACEs. Above the four ACE threshold, the data showed three times the levels of lung disease, eleven times more intervenous drug use, fourteen times more suicide attempts, four times more likely to engage in sex before the age of fifteen, five times more depression and two times more likely to get liver disease. The connection between childhood traumatic experiences and adverse adult behaviors and disease was shocking and irrefutable.

ACEs & Adverse Health Outcomes

So, how does neglect lead to, say, liver disease you might ask? It's a great question because the link does not always seem obvious. What happens is childhood traumatic experiences impact how our brains develop and our "epigenetics", how your genes are impacted by your behavior and environment. One way researchers are able to see this is through brain changes on PET scans. This kind of disrupted neurodevelopment then often leads to social, emotional, and cognitive impairments along with these physical impacts.

In addition to impacts on behavior and physical health as an adult, ACE-impacted young people also reveal social, emotional, and cognitive impairments in the school setting. For many students who have social impairments, the vast majority of the trauma was caused by other people. Because our bodies are wired for connection but also for safety, traumatized students want to connect with other people but simultaneously view others as threats. We see this play out in real time as so many of our students try over and over again to connect with other students and staff but, once those connections start to form, begin to feel unsafe and push that person away. Teachers often see this in the classroom when they start to form a quality bond with a challenging student. Just when you think you've got them figured out, they push you away with challenging behavior or self-isolate.

The piece about this that is so important, and perspective changing, is that most of this behavior is subconscious. Rather than intentionally rejecting you, their brain is pushing you away so it can feel safe. To return to our previous example, I witnessed this over and over again with Johnny as he would start to connect with his teacher and she would feel like she was finally getting "over the hump" with him. However, almost predictably, he would push her away and they would have to start the rapport building process over again.

For this reason, one of the greatest gifts we can give our students is the gift of safety. Despite how challenging it may be to feel like you are starting over gaining trust again and again, you are making an impact. In fact, you may be the first person with whom your student has ever felt safe.

Reflection Questions

1. What is your reaction to the number of traumatic experiences the ACEs study found?

2. So many of our students have been impacted by adverse childhood experiences. How is your school working to identify these students?

3. Often we will not know the specifics of students' trauma stories. What behaviors can you identify that may be an indicator of trauma?

Chapter Three

Emotional Dysregulation, "Creative" Coping, & Cognitive Impacts

"After a traumatic experience, the human system of self-preservation seems to go onto permanent alert, as if the danger might return at any moment."
~ Judith Lewis Herman

While it is possible to link many difficult student behaviors to trauma, both traumatized and untraumatized students can struggle with expressing their emotions in appropriate ways because emotional expression is a learned behavior.

The inability to manage emotions in a healthy way is known as *dysregulation*. As humans, we don't learn to self-regulate by ourselves. Rather, self-regulation is learned by receiving co-regulation over and over again from others. For example, we learn to calm down by watching other people calm down and learning from them how to do it on our own. As a parent myself, I've witnessed this thousands of times when one of my children is upset and cries until they are soothed by a parent or other caregiver.

Unfortunately, many of our students live in homes where their primary caregivers never learned how to self-regulate and, therefore, they are not modeling these important skills to their children. This is not a criticism of these parents. Instead, it is important to realize that dysregulation is passed down generationally until someone interrupts that pattern, teaching someone in the family how to recognize dysregulation and how to cope with challenging feelings. It often feels clear to teachers when they meet the parents of some of their most challenging students as they watch the parents have a hard time regulating their emotions effectively during a meeting. Seeing the parents struggling with their own self-regulation makes it clearer that the students haven't had many opportunities to practice this essential skill.

In addition to emotional dysregulation, many students with trauma histories also have resulting cognitive impairments. A myth sometimes persists that students who have been traumatized are not as intelligent as their peers. And, far too often, trauma-induced behaviors may result in an inaccurate special needs label. In reality, children who have encountered a lot of trauma are often very bright, but their traumatic experiences are preventing them from engaging effectively in school activities.

Because our bodies prioritize safety above all else, when our students have experienced extensive trauma their brains are working hard to keep them safe. Thus, they are not in the mental space needed to learn. Poignantly, Dr. Bruce Perry is quoted as saying when our students are in a state of fear their IQ drops 40 points and when they are in a state of terror it drops 50 points. Obviously, this has a significant impact on their ability in a classroom. As educators and lay-helpers in a traumatized student's life, learning how to recognize dysregulated students and helping them feel safe and connected is essential to supporting their learning ability. We will talk more extensively later in the book about why these students' brains have adapted from their trauma and how it prevents them from learning.

"Creative" Coping Skills

Students who have social, emotional, and/or cognitive impairments will creatively find ways to cope. Some of the most common ways I see middle and high school students dealing with social impairments is to engage in risky sexual behavior and unhealthy relationships and friendships. These students desperately want someone to connect with and love them so they will use sex and unhealthy relationships as a way to try to create connections. I've witnessed so many students who bounce from unhealthy relationship to unhealthy relationship as a way to try to connect with their peers. To this end, it is important to remember that for a traumatized student, a healthy relationship might feel awkward, threatening, and unfamiliar.

Similarly, students are sometimes drawn to what they know because, even if it is unhealthy, they are still more likely to predict what will happen next. Subconsciously, abused students will sometimes seek out abusive relationships because it feels predictably more "normal" and comfortable. One of the most important ways we can help students get out of abuse cycles and social impairments is to help them recognize their pattern of engaging in unhealthy relationships. This type of work is some of the most important I've done in education.

For elementary-aged students who have social, emotional, and cognitive impairments, instead of unhealthy relationships, they tend to display much more disruptive behavior. Given where they come from and what they have experienced, the foreign environment of a school can initially feel especially unfamiliar and unsafe. As trauma-informed educators, helping them feel safe and connected is one of our most important priorities. We will discuss more examples of this in the coming chapters.

Trauma-Related Emotional Impairment

Part of emotional regulation is emotional intelligence or, being able to recognize how you are feeling. For many high school-aged students who are depressed, angry, or anxious, they are unable to identify these feelings and certainly don't have the coping skills to deal with them in positive ways. As with the above "creative" coping solutions, these emotional impairments can lead to students (especially those with high ACE scores) to express their feelings in inappropriate ways; fighting, becoming verbally aggressive, shutting down, or not engaging in school at all.

In terms of gender and emotion, many boys have been raised in a hyper-masculine culture where the only safe emotion that they feel allowed to express is anger. If they express any other emotion they could be mocked, or worse. Because of this, boys tend to express a range of other difficult feelings as anger. As an example, I was amazed how many depressed boys express their sadness with anger.

Trauma-Influenced Cognitive Impairments

Lastly, students who have experienced trauma can have cognitive impairments that prevent them from being attentive throughout their educational career. For some students, they are several years behind their cohorts in math, science, and reading, partly because they get frustrated by challenging work. For these students, it often feels easier for them to act out and be removed than to feel overwhelmed, "stupid," or ashamed. With an already dysregulated sense of self, these further damaging impacts on their self-worth feel too overwhelming to face in a healthy way.

By adopting high-risk behaviors, students find creative ways to deal with their social, emotional and cognitive impairments. Unfortunately, as the ACEs study shows, these high-risk behaviors increasingly lead to disease, disability, and ultimately early death. The solution to this problem is to teach our students healthy coping skills to help them manage their stress response and equip their often lacking "coping skills toolbox."

Of course, we all utilize a variety of coping skills when our lives become challenging. However, as mentioned for our students with high ACE scores, they are often not equipped well enough with the strategies they need to deal with their struggles. As educators, if our students begin to use drugs, alcohol, vaping, and engage in risky sexual behaviors it can be upsetting. Utilizing empathy, we can acknowledge that this use may provide some relief in the short term. However, we can also point out that, long term, they are wiring their brains for addiction, relationship challenges, and potential adverse health outcomes.

No matter how they choose to cope, and the education we offer them, it is important that this is not a place for judgment. Instead, we can better understand why they make the choices they do and help guide them toward healthier options.

Reflection Questions

1. What are some of the most "creative" ways you have seen students in your school/classroom cope with dysregulation?

2. How can the generational impact of trauma help you have more empathy for the parents/family members of your students?

3. What trauma-influenced emotional or cognitive impairment do you see most often in your traumatized students?

Chapter Four

What is Trauma & How Does Trauma Wound?

"Repeated trauma requires you to create a system of defenses that protects you. And these protections were so important. They saved your life. They protected your real self." ~ Gretchen L. Schmelzer, PhD.

The dictionary describes trauma as "a deeply distressing or disturbing experience." The simplest way I describe trauma is that it is anything that overwhelms the brain's ability to cope, no matter how "big" or "small" it may seem to the outside world. We all respond to traumatic events differently, both in the moment and later on.

A common example of this can be seen in our military personnel. They fight side-by-side and yet one soldier comes home well-adjusted while another struggles with flashbacks, nightmares, and severe post-traumatic stress disorder (PTSD). It is not fully understood why some people are more intensely impacted by traumatic experiences than others.

Because of the different ways people experience trauma, when working with students, I don't focus on what they went through. As recovery from trauma is a delicate process best undertaken by a trained therapist, I instead focus my time, energy, and effort on how they are responding to challenges in their life. One of the most important things for us to realize is *even if we don't know the details of what they've experienced, we can be effective in supporting them.* Consider this concept in a personal way. Most of us have not shared the full details of our hardest experiences with many people, but we can ask ourselves how we found healthy ways to cope and understand that people have been able to help us without fully understanding the details. Many of these same processes can help our students.

Now that we've identified what trauma is, let's explore how trauma wounds us through disconnection. This includes 1) disconnecting us from ourselves, 2) from others, 3) and from a positive world view.

Disconnecting From Ourselves: One of the major ways trauma harms us is by preventing our brains from being able to recognize and control our emotions, thoughts, and behaviors in ways it did before or, in the way it was designed to. It is common for trauma survivors to have a hard time expressing their emotions the way they want to, losing control of their emotional state, lashing out, or shutting down completely. A simple analogy is when a trauma response is triggered, it is like being taken back by a time machine. Rather than experiencing what is factually going on in front of them, their brain resurfaces the same feelings they had during the traumatic event.

For many people, these kinds of vivid flashbacks put them back in that traumatic moment, possibly resurfacing the original feelings of shame, guilt, or fear that surrounds the traumatic event. Because of the intensity of these responses, those who seek to recover often struggle to express their emotions in healthy way for years. When we understand how trauma affects the brain in this way, we can see why a traumatized person fears being hurt again and may behave or express emotion in a way that does not "match" what is actually happening.

Disconnecting From Other People: As mammals, we are biologically wired to connect with others for survival. However, the problem is that in our modern world the vast majority of trauma is interpersonal, meaning the majority of our traumatized students have experienced trauma at the hands of other people. Given our primary need to connect with others, this puts our students in a very difficult situation. Their brain and biology is telling them they need to connect but their brain is also trying to achieve safety, another primary need. These competing needs means our students who have experienced trauma often view other people as threats but also feel the need to connect with them. Obviously, this is very difficult to accomplish at the same time. Part of what we will continue to explore throughout this book is how to connect with these students in a way that helps them feel both safe and connected.

Disconnecting From a Positive World View: Children who are raised in a safe, loving environment are conditioned to believe that the world is a safe place. They show up at school with the privilege of believing that everyone is safe and kind and they will learn quickly. This is much different for an abused, neglected, and/or traumatized child. When they arrive at school, their brain has been conditioned to view others as potential threats, people who could potentially hurt them. They frequently do not feel safe and will not learn optimally until they feel safe and connected with staff and peers.

As a personal example, I've seen this with my own children. Because they have experienced a healthy, safe childhood, they often come home from their first day of school and say, "I love my teacher." I remember thinking, how can you love your teacher after only one day? But, with a safe and loving environment, their brain assumes that school and teachers will be safe too. Their kindergarten teacher is kind on day one so why wouldn't they love them? In contrast, consider Johnny who showed up at kindergarten after years of neglect and abuse. His brain has been conditioned to view an adult as another person who could hurt him. Rather than entering an assumed safe experience, this new routine is likely to initially make him feel unsafe and on constant high alert.

The Most Common Traumatic Experiences

At the beginning of this chapter, we noted that a wide-variety of experiences can be traumatic events, depending on how someone experiences it. Remember, the simplest definition is that trauma is anything that overwhelms the brain's ability to cope. However, there are some common experiential pathways by which our students experience trauma. And, while this isn't a complete list, here we will explore three main categories: abuse, loss, and chronic stressors.

Abuse: Emotional, sexual, physical, domestic violence, witnessing violence, bullying

Loss: Death, abandonment, neglect, separation, natural disasters, accidents, terrorism, war

Chronic Stressors: Poverty, racism, community trauma, historical trauma, family members with substance abuse issues, domestic violence

Regarding the above categories, it is important to note that studies show that 1 out of every 3 to 4 girls will be sexually abused by the time they turn 18. The numbers for boys are 1 out of every 5 or 6, depending on which study you read. Additionally, it is important to consider that the rate for boys may actually not be that much different as they typically don't disclose their abuse to anyone for an average of 20 years. Sexual assault survivors are 10 times more likely to use hard drugs.

In addition to abuse, domestic violence is also an epidemic in our society. One out of every four homes has severe domestic violence. That means 25% of our students don't go home to a safe place every night. Having a safe home is essential for reducing our stress levels, a process that is important for all people but especially our students whose brains have been traumatized.

As an example of how safety impacts the brain, consider a bunny rabbit hopping around your backyard. That bunny spends its entire day hyper-aware, trying not to be eaten by coyotes, hawks, dogs, or cats. While stressed several times throughout its day, at the end of the day it goes home to its burrow and nestles next to its bunny family and relaxes. It has a place to reduce its stress for a time until it enters the world again. Contrast that visual with a student like Johnny living in an abusive home. Instead of being able to relax, when he returns home he does not know if he will be met with anger or violence. His body and brain remain on constant high alert waiting for the next traumatic moment. As human beings we all need a home where we can feel safe and relax at the end of the day, allowing our brains to heal from the intensity of the day. Unfortunately, our students who are growing up in abusive and violent homes do not have that safe place to go to everyday. Those constant high levels of stress damage their bodies, mental health, relationships, and coping skills.

While it can be difficult to consider these statistics, it is important for us to remember what a portion of our students face every day. When I travel to speak about trauma-informed care I hear over and over again, "What's wrong with kids these days?" But, when we remember what so many of them have and are encountering we can realize there's nothing "wrong" with these kids. Instead, there is something wrong with their environment. We are better helpers when we remember their behavior makes sense when we take their environment into context.

Reflection Questions

1. What are two ways you see your students disconnect from others?

2. How can we help our most challenging students connect in healthy ways both with students and staff?

3. What are ways that we can help students feel safer in our school so they can connect better?

Chapter Five

Trauma's Impact on Educational Outcomes

"A good teacher isn't someone who gives the answers out to their kids but is understanding of needs and challenges and gives tools to help other people succeed."
~ Justin Trudeau

While we briefly explored the impact of trauma on a student's education via the ACE study, in this chapter we will consider this more in depth. Today's educational environment requires schools and teachers to undertake significant evaluation measures. Unfortunately, I've seen many schools suspend regular instruction and spend their entire spring semester preparing students to take EOC exams or ACT tests. As a trauma-informed specialist, I believe far too many schools make training their students on standardized tests their primary mission and goal. There must be a better partnership between the direction of education and the needs of *all* students. If we want students to perform better on these tests we must understand the impact childhood trauma has on their learning.

Regarding learning and education, childhood trauma adversely affects a child's ability to:

- Acquire language and communications skills
- Understand cause and effect
- Take another person's perspective
- Attend regular classroom instruction
- Engage in curriculum
- Utilize executive functions
- Make plans
- Organize work
- Follow classroom rules
(Wolopow, et al., 2009)

With the challenges listed above it's no wonder that we have so many students struggling academically. Additional impacts of childhood trauma effects on school performance include:

- Lower scores on standardized achievement tests (Goodman et al., 2011)
- Substantial decreases in IQ, reading achievement and language (Delaney-Blacket et al., 2002)
- 30-fold increase in learning or behavior problems (as reported by parents) between children with high ACE scores (4+) compared to children with no ACEs (Webster, 2002)

The original (and often ongoing) structure of our educational system was not designed to support children who have been impacted by trauma. Untraumatized students come to school, often have very few behavioral issues, learn, and graduate. In contrast, our traumatized students have been historically met with suspension, expulsion, and approximately 13% don't graduate from high school. Interestingly, this is very close to the same percentage of students who have an ACE score of 4 or more.

For far too long our school systems' only answer to trauma-influenced behavior has been suspension and expulsion, thus reinforcing the trauma these students have experienced. We need to do better, finding ways to be part of the solution, not part of the problem. I am excited to share some of these strategies in the coming chapters but, until then, let's check back in with Johnny's story.

"Johnny Lashes Out"

We pick back up in Johnny's story in February of his kindergarten year. In his grandmother's loving, supportive home, Johnny was doing much better. And, while his first semester was a daily challenge for his teacher, counselor, and principal, his behavior at school was starting to improve. By February,

Johnny started to feel safer at school, building strong bonds with his teacher and counselor. His teacher met him with consistent, unconditional love everyday despite his challenging behaviors and never gave up on him when his behaviors made her job much more difficult. And, with the social skills work he was doing with his school counselor, he even began to make and maintain some friendships by dealing with conflict in healthy ways, taking turns, and being polite.

While still far behind academically, Johnny's teacher was working hard to close the gaps and showed me his tremendous progress. Despite all that he had been through, I felt a tremendous sense of pride in working with this little boy who was finally getting the support he needed and traveling on a path of recovery.

One February morning, Johnny was sitting at a table talking and playing with his friends when his school counselor came up behind him and tapped him on the shoulder. Instantly, Johnny turned around and punched the counselor in the face, hitting him so hard in the nose that it began to bleed. This resulted in the phone call no mental health professional wants to get.

The principal called and said we needed to have an emergency meeting. The point of the meeting was to decide if Johnny needed to be suspended or expelled, even talking about the possibility of using the Safe Schools Act to remove Johnny for the rest of the year.

It was a hard call to receive. Because, while safety in schools is important for students, sadly, I've seen this legislation used to remove children as young as kindergartners for violations as small as throwing small rocks on the playground. In almost every case, removing a child from school for an entire school year is devastating to their development and often lands them back in an environment where they are further traumatized. By removing them for long periods of time they lose that safe haven and experience more trauma in their home environment.

With all the progress he had made, I was so concerned for this little boy. My past experiences told me that when children in foster care get kicked out of school for the entire year they typically end up in residential facilities for 6-18 months. These facilities often have high staff turnover and the children are removed from the positive relationships they may have had in their home and/or school environments. Despite positive efforts, when we send children to these facilities, we rarely get positive outcomes. And, as we've discussed, novelty is very difficult for children whose brains have been conditioned to assume threat in their environment. Traumatized children need consistent safe loving relationships in order to thrive and heal. By the temporary nature of their design, these facilities by design do not provide foundational emotional needs for these children.

Reflection Questions

1. What ideas do you have to help with the tension between EOC/standardized testing and meeting the needs of all students?

2. What is your initial reaction to the story about Johnny lashing out?

Chapter Six

This is Your Brain on Trauma

"Trauma causes us to have an internal experience that is frightening, angry, and shameful. When we feel threatened, as we do when we are traumatized, our entire organism is geared up to find the source of that threat and to do something about it."~ Peter A. Levine

In chapter four we addressed the definition of trauma, where it most commonly stems from for our students, and how it impacts disconnection from self, others, and a positive world view. As a continuation of that discussion, we will now consider more of the science and brain structure related to trauma. I truly enjoy taking complex neuroscience and simplifying it so we can understand and apply it to our own lives and the lives of our students.

Understanding trauma at its most basic level is as simple as identifying the front of the brain and the back of the brain. The front of our brains is the most evolved organ of any animal on the planet. It is the part that controls functions such as emotional expression, problem solving, memory, and judgment. It is what has allowed us to become the apex creature on the planet. With it, we solve complex math equations, understand science, build cities, bridges, cathedrals, and make amazing music and art. And, while all of this is incredible, this section of the brain does have a few areas of susceptibility. It is the slowest part of the brain to develop, not often being fully wired until we are in our mid-20's and, it is the first thing to slow or shut down in a crisis.

For this reason, as humans, we are fortunate to have a survival-based back of the brain. This part of the brain controls many of our basic, automatic functions like breathing, swallowing, heart rate, blood pressure, etc.. Unlike the front part of the brain that thinks through rationale and options, the back of the brain responds automatically for survival with only three options: fight, flight, and freeze.

In addition to this, we also have a "smoke detector" of sorts in the middle of the brain called the amygdala. In this way, the amygdala's job is to sense life or death situations, setting off the "smoke detector." When this happens, the front of the brain slows or shuts down and the back of the brain takes control, triggering it to fight, flight, or freeze. But, why does it do this? Wouldn't it be best to keep the rational, front part of our brain functioning in a crisis? Perhaps not. Consider this example.

Bears & Bombs

If a bear bursts into the room, you would not want the front of your brain to be in charge. You wouldn't want to stop and think, "Why is this bear in here? What does this bear want? Is my insurance going to cover the damage from the bear? Will my friends think I'm a coward for running from the bear?" In fact, if our brains worked this way, our ancestors would have all been eaten by saber tooth tigers in caves hundreds of thousands of years ago. Our front brain is simply too evolved to keep us safe when we need to survive.

Instead, when a bear bursts into the room our smoke detector goes off, shutting down the front of the brain and the survival-based back of the brain takes over. In this moment, your brain will then choose to fight, flight, or freeze, whichever it thinks will keep you the safest. I can't emphasize this enough, once we are triggered to the back of the brain we don't get to choose our response. And, this is part of what is so important to understand about our students who have experienced trauma. Because of their experiences, the front of their brains are less developed and quickly shut down when they encounter a real *or perceived* threat. The back of the brain does not have consciousness, it is automatic. So, when we're triggered to the back of the brain we lose rational control and have autonomic responses, not being able to choose if we fight, flight, or freeze.

As another example, you may have heard of the police officer in Florida who stayed in his police car during a school shooting. This officer heard gunshots ringing out through the school building, and yet he sat in his car and didn't respond to the deadly situation. At the time I was writing this book that officer was being charged for a crime for not responding, which may instinctively feel reasonable. However, let's examine what possibly happened when the officer heard gunshots.

His "smoke detector" went off because this was a life or death situation. The back of the brain was triggered and he had a freeze response. If this is the case, He didn't choose that freeze response and he didn't have control over that freeze response. Instead, that freeze response kept him completely still in his car. The back of his brain was in control and he couldn't move. And, while this is a modern day example, I'm a lover of history and in every battle in the history of mankind there are examples of soldiers who have fight, flight, or freeze responses. In particular, WWI was especially cruel and many soldiers on both sides were executed for "cowardice" but, in reality, they were soldiers who experienced a freeze response.

Now, for those wondering how we have soldiers and police officers and examples throughout history of people who did not experience this back-of-brain response, it is important to note that we can *learn* to remain engaged with the front of our brains, thus avoiding fight, flight, or freeze responses. One of the best strategies for this is to avoid being triggered in the first place by controlling our heart rate.

As I've traveled the country, I've trained hundreds of police officers on the "Navy Seals Method" of controlled breathing, also called "square breathing." Navy Seals consistently encounter life-or-death situations but it is essential that they also maintain control in the front of their brain. Square breathing allows them to keep their heart rate lowered and keep themselves from being triggered to back-of-brain control with a fight, flight, or freeze response.

As effective as it is, you would think square breathing would be complicated. It is not. Simply breathe in for four seconds, hold it for four seconds, exhale for four seconds and pause for four seconds. This method of square breathing allows you to control your heart rate and keep yourself from losing access to the front of the brain. And, of course, I wouldn't share it with you if it were only effective for Navy Seals. This tool can be used by educators and students alike. Anytime you find yourself in a stressful situation, square breathing can help you keep calm and keep you in the front of your brain where you have more logical, rational thought and control.

"Smoke Detector" Memory

As we continue forward in understanding how trauma affects our brains, it's important to know that our amygdala "smoke detectors" also remember every single life or death experience we've ever had, in detail. So, your "smoke detector" remembers everything you tasted, touched, smelled, saw, or heard during threatening experiences in order to retain and use that information to keep you safe in future experiences. In fact, your "smoke detector" doesn't remember these traumatic experiences as a conscious thought but, instead, as a sensory experience.

Remember the bear example? Let's return to that. If you had formerly been traumatized by a bear and then years later heard a bear growl, your "smoke detector" would go off and send you into an automatic response. But, if you only smelled the bear, your "smoke detector" would also go off. Similarly, if you heard a bear scratching the door, the same would occur.. As a species, you can see how this response has previously been very advantageous to us. We don't actually have to encounter the threat to move into a life saving fight, flight, or freeze response. In this example, our ancestors would be able to run away from the bear before they ever saw it, using their senses as an early warning system to greatly increase their chances of survival. It's an obvious advantage for people living for survival in a harsh natural world thousands of years ago. But, this same biological design can make our modern human relationships more challenging.

A Look Inside a Traumatized Brain

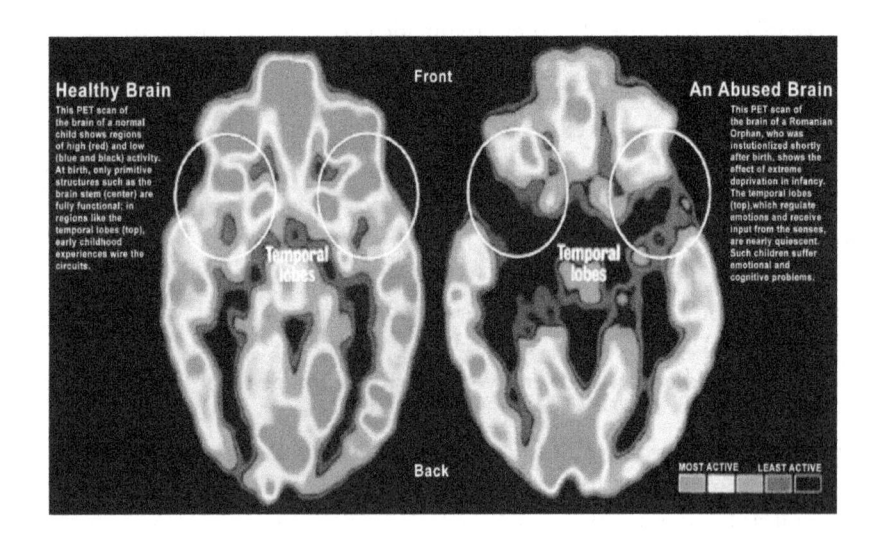

Healthy Brain
This PET scan of the brain of a normal child shows regions of high (red) and low (blue and black) activity. At birth, only primitive structures such as the brain stem (center) are fully functional; in regions like the temporal lobes (top), early childhood experiences wire the circuits.

An Abused Brain
This PET scan of the brain of a Romanian Orphan, who was institutionized shortly after birth, shows the effect of extreme deprivation in infancy. The temporal lobes (top), which regulate emotions and receive input from the senses, are nearly quiescent. Such children suffer emotional and cognitive problems.

Every single experience we have either wires us to engage the front or the back of our brains. In this picture, we can see that when a child is in a safe and loving environment they develop strong neural connections to the front of their brain. When human beings live in safe supportive environments, they can spend the majority of their lives accessing the front of the brain, learning and growing throughout their lives. This allows us to accomplish great things and solve incredible problems. In contrast, as you can see with the traumatized child (on the right), when you grow up in an unhealthy, non-nurturing, or abusive environment there are less connections and access to the front of the brain.

Children who experience chronic trauma spend most of their lives in the back of the brain where they can't learn well and have great difficulty reacting rationally. The only thing the back of the brain can do is fight, flight, or freeze. Some people in dangerous neighborhoods or war torn countries spend most of their lives living out of the back of their brains, constantly in a reactionary state of fight, flight, or freeze responses. Additionally, consider this. Human beings are only 5% wired at birth. The additional wiring is 95% a reflection of our environment and will adapt to survive in the situations we experience. That is why schools are the most impactful place for young traumatized people to heal. When we simply consider the numbers, we get these kids in our schools for approximately 13 years, 8 hours a day. What an opportunity to help repair and rewire their brains in a healthy way.

Johnny's Response: An Application

At this point, we return to Johnny and the incident when he punched the counselor. If you walk up behind a child who has not experienced trauma and tap them on the shoulder they will most likely turn around and say, "Hi." But, Johnny's amygdala or "smoke detector" had experienced so many traumatic moments when he lived with his methamphetamine-addicted mother that when touched from behind, his amygdala or "smoke detector" sprang into action. It remembered that when someone touches you unexpectedly from behind they are there to hurt you. The front of his brain turned off and the back of his brain chose a fight response, resulting in his counselor being punched.

For some mental health professionals, this is labeled a "maladaptive response." I avoid this term because it suggests that the response is bad, implying the kid is "bad." And, while it is not an option for Johnny to continue to assault people at school, when considering a response, all those caring for Johnny must remember that this brain response is part of what helped keep this little boy alive all those years when he had no one to protect him. At the time, it was not maladaptive, it was life saving.

When I arrived that day for the emergency meeting, I'll never forget the look in the school counselor's eyes. Both of his nostrils were packed with tissues. He said to me, "How could that boy punch me in the face? I love that boy and he loves me." His pain was understandable. As we sat around the table, I explained about the front of the brain, back of the brain, the amygdala, and how Johnny's "smoke detector" was over-reactive because of all the trauma he experienced. It was incredible to watch the room change from talk about the "Safe Schools Act" and "expulsions" to "what has that boy been through" and "how can we support him." I was so grateful for their willingness to consider an alternative perspective.

In order to best meet the needs of traumatized children, this is the type of conversational transformation that has to happen to every school in the United States. We have to stop saying, "What is wrong with that child?" and start saying, "What happened to that child?" and "What can I do to help?" The destructive behavior we're seeing all over this country from our students makes complete sense when we consider their life experiences. Our students' aggression, defiance, and withdrawing behaviors make sense once we understand what's going on inside their brains. And, as radical as it may sound, with the right support, all of these kids can be successful. They can grow into healthy productive adults. This life-saving transformation is why I'm so passionate about sharing this message.

Reflection Questions

1. How does the explanation of how the front and the back of the brain operate during trauma help you as an educator?

2. Offer a personal example you have experienced or witnessed when someone reacted with fight, flight, or freeze.

3. Following the story about Johnny's school's response, has your initial reaction to his outburst changed? If so, in what way?

Chapter Seven

Fight, Flight, & Freeze in a School Setting

"After a traumatic experience, the human system of self-preservation seems to go onto permanent alert, as if the danger might return at any moment."
~ Judith Lewis Herman

To this point, we have explored the concept of trauma, brain science, and how this played out so far in Johnny's life. In this chapter, we are going to get more personal, exploring what fight, flight and freeze responses might look like for students in our classrooms. As we begin, recall that every time a traumatized student is triggered, they can be involuntarily moved into a flight, flight, or freeze state. You can notice this by impulsive reactions and emotional dysregulation. Thus, as we learn to identify these dysregulated students by their behavior, we can learn to support them instead of immediately moving to punishment and removal.

"Fight"

Let's explore what the fight response might look like in a classroom. While some students get into physical altercations as a result of their overactive fight response, I also regularly see verbal aggression in these students. The unconscious back-of-the-brain fight responses are designed to keep people at a safe distance. As a method of protection, if a student can push you away or push themselves out of the class or even the school, they'll often feel safer.

In addition to physical or verbal aggression, I also see the fight response expressed in the form of hypervigilance or hyperactivity. A traumatized student's brain doesn't experience school as a safe place. When they sit down in a classroom their brain is on high alert, instinctively trying to identify the next potential threat. These students often have a hard time sitting still, paying attention, and they may constantly look around the room. These examples reflect common fight responses as the brains of our students try to achieve safety.

Of course, these are also the types of behaviors that end up involving treatment or mental health care. However, far too often mental health professionals may not take the client's life history into context when making a diagnosis, instead misdiagnosing these traumatized students with attention-deficit and/or hyperactivity disorders instead of a more accurate diagnosis of PTSD (Post Traumatic Stress Disorder). This was the case for Johnny. Rather than recognizing that when he showed up to school, his brain was constantly searching the room for threats, he was instead quickly diagnosed with ADHD and put on stimulants.

"Flight"

As I saw with Johnny, as educators, we may see many flight responses in the classroom. A common one for elementary students is to run away. However, for middle and high school students it is often disconnecting, isolation, and avoidance. Remember, the vast majority of these students were traumatized by other people so it makes sense for their brain to keep them safe by keeping other people away. Isolation may look like not talking to anyone, sitting alone, or putting their hoodie up. By distancing themselves from other students and school staff, they unconsciously feel they are safer from future pain. For some students, this protection takes the form of the physical distancing mentioned or emotional distancing where they may seem close but once the relationship starts to form they will disengage.

"Freeze"

Lastly, let's talk about freeze responses in the school setting. One common freeze response is when students look dazed and sleepy, especially in stressful situations. It is a way of dissociating as a way to deal with their emotional pain. It's like checking out of your own body. It's a very numbing feeling. These students will look like they are not paying attention or will simply put their head down. Another manifestation of this is self-harm or "cutting." Cutting provides a temporary relief from the numb feeling because pain-induced endorphins are released as a result of their cutting. As uncomfortable as cutting may seem to us, the positive feelings they get from these endorphins are why it is so difficult for students to stop cutting once that unhealthy coping strategy is established.

While we have not discussed it thus far, "fawning" behavior is also another trauma response. To keep things simple, I like to put the fawn response under the freeze category. Many trauma survivors have learned that the best way to stay safe is to do what others want us to do. By "fawning", if they put others' needs before their own they are less likely to be harmed and have a greater chance of establishing a safe-feeling connection with others. These people become experts at reading others and predicting their needs so they have a better chance of being safe. You may recognize this trauma response in students who are doing everything they can to make you and others happy, going so far as to engage in behavior that is not in their best interest in an attempt to meet these needs.

Changing Our Response in Education

Far too often in education, when we come across these children using the "back of the brain," we meet them with punishment and shame. However, we are not helping these students be successful by making them feel worse about themselves. And, we cannot best help these students by removing them from our school community. This has been tried for decades and failed. I believe this is a significant factor why, on average, 13% of our students do not graduate high school. If we don't help these students heal, their pain will continue to be passed down to their children, as we all learn to parent by being parented.

I honestly believe most parents are doing the best they can. In fact, this perspective helps me be a more compassionate educator. But, when the parents of our students were not raised in a healthy environment it is very challenging to create that environment for their own children if they haven't healed. The answer to this problem is not punishment, shame, and disconnection. Instead, it is love and connection. When we support these students and help them heal by teaching them how to regulate their stress response, they will then have the opportunity to pass this down to their children and our next generations will be far more regulated.

Reflection Questions

1. Describe what a fight, flight, or freeze situation looked like for a student in your school.

2. How can you personally change your response to students who are in "the back of the brain?"

Chapter 8

Triggers

"Your triggers are pathways to your wounds. The stimulus is only a door." ~ *Sanhita Baruah*

Now that we have discussed what trauma reactions might look like, it is important to consider what "triggers" them. In short, triggers can be any sensory information. Remember, the amygdala ("smoke detector") stores all the sensory information from previous traumatic events and will transport the person to the back of the brain when the same sensory information is presented again in order to keep them safe. It should be noted, sometimes these triggers are easy to identify and sometimes it can be very challenging.

Anytime the stressor and response are not in alignment we must consider trauma as the source of the behavior.

For example, if you are enjoying the Fourth of July fireworks and you see an Army Veteran run away at the first sound of the fireworks it is possible to see the soldier may have experienced trauma without ever saying a word to him. His response (running) does not match up with his stressor (fireworks) so we can consider that the cause of the behavior may be a traumatic experience. If this is the case, that soldier's amygdala senses the concussion sound and remembers the sounds of war. He is then triggered into the back of the brain and has a flight response as a way to try to achieve safety.

One way I commonly observe this in the school setting is when two students bump into each other in the hallway. Typically, one student understands that these bumps are a normal part of navigating busy hallways. However, to a traumatized student that bump can feel like an attack. I've interviewed dozens of students who believe they were "attacked" during one of these simple interactions. Normally, I'll look at the video and see it's an unintentional bump. But when I interview the student they'll describe in great detail how they were minding their own business and were suddenly attacked. In these cases, the students' amygdala's "smoke detectors" are being set off and they are having a fight response. Of course, this doesn't mean we don't hold these students accountable for their behavior. However, it does help to understand the root of the behavior so we can work to change it. Again, anytime the stressor and response are not in alignment we must consider trauma is the source of the behavior. We need to learn to ask ourselves, "What is the root of this irrational behavior?"

Triggered: A Personal Example

Several years ago, my daughter Claire was flagged by the school nurse for failing her vision test. My wife, Ashley, took Claire to the optometrist and got her vision checked and bought a new pair of glasses to correct her vision. Claire came home so excited to show her Dad her new glasses. They were pink with a cute bow in the corner. She said, "Look Dad! I have glasses like you! I'm so lucky!" I was happy to celebrate with her. However, my wife's reaction was different. Upset, she said, "Why does Claire need to have glasses, it's not fair?" I found myself irritated by her comment, thinking, "What's the big deal?" Then my wife said, "First asthma and now glasses. It's just not fair." I grew in my frustration saying, "Honey, there is nothing wrong with people with glasses." pointing at my own. As she was still upset I grew in my frustration until I said, "I don't know if you know how genetics work, but I had glasses on our first date, what did you think was going to happen?" I admit, it wasn't my best moment.

After taking a few moments to calm down (and re-engage the front of my brain!), I had an epiphany. I started thinking about what I taught all those educators over the years: *If the response doesn't equal the stressor, think trauma.* I asked my wife if she had ever been to the optometrist before (she doesn't wear glasses). She said, "When I was seven years old my Mom died and I had a lazy eye. They took me to the optometrist and he put drops in my eyes and it stung and I cried and cried and no one was there to comfort me." Thirty years later my wife walked back into the optometrist and her amygdala or "smoke detector" hadn't forgotten. She was transported back to all those feelings of being a scared and lonely seven-year-old girl. That's how powerful your "smoke detector" is. That's how important it is to your brain to keep you safe. As soon as my wife got the opportunity to understand the root of these feelings and express them she was fine. Anytime the stressor and response are not in alignment we must consider trauma as the source of the behavior.

Common School-Setting Triggers

It is important to work together to identify triggers for our students because, if we can figure out what is triggering them, then we can either remove the trigger or help them to cope. Per the previous example, it was very easy for me to remove my wife's trigger for the optometrist. I'll take our daughter to the optometrist next time. However, in school settings it may be more complicated. Let's explore some of the more common school-setting triggers.

One of the most common events that can trigger traumatized students is breaking routine. In general, people thrive when they have a consistent routine. But, for people who have experienced trauma, it feels much more unsafe if they can not predict what is coming next. As a trauma-informed school, keeping your routine as close to the same as possible everyday is supportive for your students. This helps them stay in the front of the brain where they can learn and thrive.

Hallway time is also a common trigger for students. Many of our hallways are packed with students and it's no wonder that traumatized students don't feel safe. If a student is struggling with peer interaction in the hallway, you may want to consider giving them a few minutes before or after class to move to class in a less chaotic environment. Adjusting their passing time is a simple way to help them feel safer.

Another very common trigger for many people is rejection. When students reject each other it can cause a triggered response. Our students' access to social media has made this trigger much more frequent. I sometimes joke that if Snapchat didn't exist I wouldn't have a job. Rejection from staff is also a common trigger when we are using traditional punishment techniques like shame and/or isolation. We need to work together to make sure we are being supportive to our students even when we don't like their behavior. We can address the behavior without rejecting the person. For example, if a student is constantly answering questions out of turn, we can talk to that student in private and explain that we love how engaged they are in the material but want to give other students an opportunity to show what they've learned. That way we're correcting the behavior without pushing the student away.

Loud places and large groups are also common school triggers. Once again, the student's brain is trying to keep them safe and they can't feel safe when they're overwhelmed by the large crowds and noisy environment. I've accommodated many students over the years by giving them a quiet place to eat lunch or by allowing them to not attend assemblies. During the Covid-19 pandemic, my school had socially-distanced lunches, thus limiting the number of students in the lunchroom. Interestingly, we found that with a less loud and chaotic lunchroom our behavioral issues during lunch and immediately after plummeted.

On a personal note, throughout my career in education, I've noticed that I can trigger students just by being a large male. Male staff need to understand that the vast majority of physical violence is perpetrated by males. Many of our students can be triggered just by our physical size or the lower tones of our voices. Being a male in a school can be a big advantage because so many students lack father figures and they tend to gravitate towards males to have their need for fathers figures fulfilled. But, we need to recognize that we can trigger many of our students by yelling or even using a stern tone. I try to be very conscious of how proximity to me makes students feel and/or how they respond to the sound of my voice.

If a student tends to be triggered by male teachers, it can be helpful to partner with female staff members to make sure we are meeting the emotional needs of those students. Just because students may be triggered by my size and voice doesn't mean that I cannot help them. In fact, I think the inverse is true. I have a unique opportunity to retrain their brain so that males can be safe people but I need to do this in ways that consider their trauma responses and triggers until we build that relationship.

As mentioned early in this chapter, sometimes triggers are very difficult to identify. I once worked with a high school girl who was sexually assaulted in the rain. It took awhile but eventually we figured out that any time it rained she would be triggered. So whenever I was driving into work and it was raining, she would come into my office to do a self regulating activity before going to class so that she could calm down and focus enough to learn. She could then learn better because her fight, flight, or freeze response was calmed by her coping strategies. I share this story to encourage you to be patient and understand that even though it can take awhile to unlock these puzzles, when you do it can be life changing.

Remember, triggers can be any sensory information. Get to know your students and work with your colleagues to figure out what is triggering them. Once you find the trigger either remove it or teach the student to cope with it. Most importantly, remember the behavior is not personal. *They are not giving you a hard time, they are having a hard time.* Keep your cool and be an investigator trying to figure out the cause. The brain is always thinking safety first.

Hero Spotlight: Barb Martin & Stephanie Moats

I once worked with a 3rd grade girl who was severely traumatized. If we brought a substitute teacher into her classroom she would tear the room apart. She didn't feel safe with her routine being disturbed and had a massive fight response to try to achieve safety. Fortunately, this girl had a loving and empathetic teacher named Stephanie Moats. She also had an incredible principal, Barb Martin. It would have been easy for these educators to remove this girl from their school community because of her erratic behavior. Instead, Mrs. Moats poured into this girl everyday. She taught this little girl what it meant to receive consistent love and care. Ms. Martin would constantly evaluate what was working and what support this girl needed to be successful. She felt that so many people had already failed this child and her school was not going to be another failure.

In an effort to help with this young girl's triggers, they decided to bring the substitute teacher in the day before they would be teaching. The substitute teacher and the teacher would sit down with the girl and explain what the next day would look like. When they did this, she would typically have a good day with the substitute teacher. Taking the time to make sure the student would be comfortable with disrupting her routine was essential for her to be successful. These kinds of intentional choices can be a great help for our traumatized students.

Hero Spotlight: Michelle Oliver

My friend Michelle was a high school librarian. I was blessed to be able to work with her for four years. She created an amazing, loving, and warm environment in her library for her students. If you visited the school you would find that many students found their "home" in her library. She constantly checked in on their emotional health, celebrated their big moments, and was there to support them during difficult days. Several times each month she would uncover a serious mental health concern and walk the student up to my office to make sure their needs were being met. Michelle is a wonderful example of a support staff member who utilized her unique role and space in the school to create a safe environment for students.

Reflection Questions

1. What support systems can we provide for our students to remove them from their triggers?

2. What in your current school environment or routine feels like it might be a trigger for students?

Chapter 9

Three Types of Stress & the Body's Response

"It isn't the mountain ahead that wears you out; it's the grain of sand in your shoe." ~ Robert W. Service

As much as we have talked about our students' traumatic stress reactions, not all stress is bad. In fact, there are three types of stress: positive, tolerable, and toxic. Positive stress is a temporary and mild increase in our stress response. Athletes call this being in the "zone." A mild amount of stress actually helps us be more energetic and alert. When I speak in front of an audience, I experience positive stress and it helps keep my brain sharp and my energy level high. After I'm done speaking I often feel fatigued. Positive stress does not have long lasting effects on our bodies and does not require someone else to help us cope.

However, the other two types of stress are not healthy. Tolerable or toxic stress refers to consistent and repetitive high levels of stress. Students who have a trusting caring adult in their life will be more likely to manage that high level of stress and it will become tolerable. Students without a trusting caring loving adult will more likely end up with toxic stress.

Toxic stress is the type people may refer to as a "killer", leading to all sorts of physical health, mental health, and addiction issues. In a perfect world, all of our students would be equipped with a parent who could provide them with a loving, caring relationship that would teach them how to manage their stress response. But, we don't live in a perfect world and we don't work at perfect schools. Many of our students don't have an adult in their life who knows how to manage their own stress responses. If, as parents, they are unable to manage their own stress response, then they can't teach their children to do it.

Some of the parents we work with use drugs and alcohol as an attempt to manage their stress response system. I never blame parents. The vast majority of parents I've worked with are doing the best they can with the tools they were given. Trauma cascades down generation to generation until the proper support is given for the healing to occur. The good news is that you can be the trusting, caring adult in your students' life. I've talked to trauma survivors all over the country and they always point out one person who made a huge impact in their life such as a coach, a teacher, an uncle, a friend who was there for them. Research has proven over and over again that *every trauma survivor is just one caring, loving relationship away from being a success story*. This is why so many of you went into education, to be that person who makes a lifelong impact. It's my hope that this book gives you a few more tools to build those meaningful relationships.

Many books and programs claim that we can teach students to be "gritty" or resilient. However, the research is clear that we don't learn how to be resilient. Resiliency is something that results from having close, healthy relationships. The more secure our attachment is with other human beings the more resilient we become. Human beings can go through unimaginably difficult experiences if they have the right love and support from strong relationships. If we want to make an impact on the traumatized students in our school then we have to get serious about forming great relationships with them. We will talk more about attachment later in this book.

Hero Spotlight: Victor Bell

Victor is a Social Studies teacher and coach. Vic is the only teacher I've ever been jealous of. I was jealous that almost every kid in the building would light up when they walked past him in the halls. Watching those faces light up as he says hi, or when he gets excited about one of their recent accomplishments was something I got to witness everyday. I've never worked with anyone who connected with so many students. He was able to connect with so many students because of his constant positive attitude, infectious smile, and laugh. He worked hard everyday to learn about his students' struggles and celebrate their triumphs. Thousands of students are more resilient and more gritty because they had Victor Bell as their teacher. His legacy is truly immeasurable.

The Body's Response to Stress

Our bodies have a significant response every time the smoke detector is triggered because the brain is telling the body to prepare for survival. And, while we've talked about this way this process operates in our brains, it also extends to the rest of our bodies. In these times, the body shuts down anything associated with long-term care to use all of its resources for a short-term threat. These may include slowing or shutting down digestion, cell repair, and sex reproduction. As an example, it's important to consider trauma as a possibility for younger students who complain that their stomach hurts all the time. Unless there is a medical issue, it is possible to consider that they can't verbalize trauma that they may have experienced but they can verbalize the pain they are experiencing from the disruptions in their digestive system.

Some other interesting things the body does when triggered include the lungs taking in more oxygen to fight off this threat and the liver dumping large amounts of glucose into the bloodstream to give energy to fight or run. The adrenal glands will produce adrenaline and cortisol to help us deal with inflammation and pain. Additionally, blood pressure rises and blood is diverted from the extremities into our core. Our bodies also produce endorphins which help us ignore pain.

As you might imagine from this list, the huge mobilization that the body does to increase the chance of survival has an impact on the individual. These physical reactions can make a person feel stressed, dizzy, out of breath, shaky, or just unsafe. This is the kind of experience our traumatized students have when they are triggered several times a day. Their bodies are going through this stress response repeatedly. It's no wonder that they seek out unhealthy coping methods to deal with this severe problem. Imagine getting in your car and alternately stomping the gas and stomping the brakes everywhere you go day after day. Of course, your car will have engine problems, transmission issues, brake failure, etc. This is why so many untreated trauma survivors have so many negative health outcomes. This constant stress response is harmful to our physical bodies long term.

As an example from our ongoing case study, Johnny constantly complained about stomach aches. He would also go from being hypervigilant for several days to shutting down for a day. During his hypervigilant days he couldn't sit still and he would constantly scan the room. When he was hypovigilant he would just put his head down and he would have a glazed over look on his face and sometimes sleep. These were all clear signs that he was struggling with his stress response system that had real impacts on his body. All students are going to encounter a combination of positive and toxic stress at different points in their lives but, it is the toxic stress especially where we can really help our students learn to cope. We will explore practical ways to do this in later chapters.

Reflection Questions

1. What does your body feel like when you are hyper-aroused? Hypo-aroused?

2. In what ways can you tell that you have moved from positive stress to toxic stress? Consider behaviors, body sensations, etc.

Chapter 10

Stuck On, Stuck Off

"Trauma causes us to have an internal experience that is frightening, angry, and shameful. When we feel threatened, as we do when we are traumatized, our entire organism is geared up to find the source of that threat and to do something about it." ~ Peter A. Levine

When the body has undischarged traumatic stress, it can lead them to be "stuck on" or "stuck off" to cope. The below illustration shows what the body does with undischarged traumatic stress. The area in between the dotted lines is known as the "window of tolerance." This is a fancy term for, "I'm in control of my emotions and behaviors." Some people develop a very large "window of tolerance." They can go through very stressful situations and stay calm and under control. However, children who've experienced extensive trauma tend to have a smaller "window of tolerance." For them, even the smallest inconvenience can cause them to lose control over their emotions and behaviors by acting out or shutting down.

Symptoms of Un-Discharged Traumatic Stress

Traumatic Event

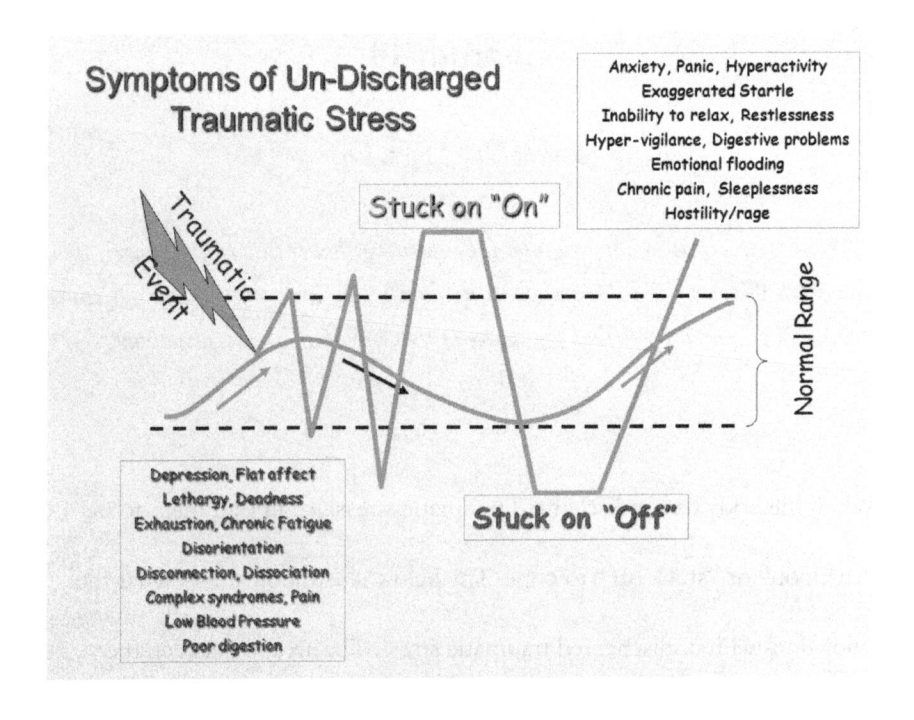

Stuck on "On"

Anxiety, Panic, Hyperactivity
Exaggerated Startle
Inability to relax, Restlessness
Hyper-vigilance, Digestive problems
Emotional flooding
Chronic pain, Sleeplessness
Hostility/rage

Normal Range

Depression, Flat affect
Lethargy, Deadness
Exhaustion, Chronic Fatigue
Disorientation
Disconnection, Dissociation
Complex syndromes, Pain
Low Blood Pressure
Poor digestion

Stuck on "Off"

As you can see in the diagram, the gray line is a well regulated person. They have their ups and downs throughout the day but stay within their "window of tolerance" and maintain control through coping skills. For example, if I get cut off by another driver going to work I might get angry, but I don't lose control and get out of my car to instigate a fight. If my son refuses to sleep at night, I might be very tired in the morning, but I'm still in control and I get up and go to work. Because our traumatized students do not have the coping skills they need and have a smaller window of tolerance, it is harder for them to remain in the healthy range.

"Stuck On": When we experience traumatic events, our body responds by putting us on high alert. This high alert response is designed to keep us safe and help us identify potential threats. In our students, this hyper-vigilance state may look like being restless. They can't sit still, can't focus on the schoolwork, have a hard time regulating emotions, and experience panic and anxiety. This hypervigilant behavior requires a tremendous amount of energy. For those who are "stuck on" for a while, they will eventually crash into hypo-vigilance (low energy).

"Stuck Off": This hypo-vigilence (low energy) looks like being disengaged, tired, checked out, defiant, and dissociated. Additionally, some students will cycle back and forth between hyper and hypo vigilant states quite quickly while others will be stuck in one state or the other more dominantly.

Trauma Mimics Other Mental Health Disorders

Far too often in the mental health world we've been quick to diagnose hyper-vigilant kids as ADHD or ADD. This diagnosis is only appropriate if the child does not have a traumatic history. If mental health professionals do not consider the patient's life circumstances when making a diagnosis, they will only be able to base the diagnosis on the current behaviors and level of functioning instead of on the experiences the client has lived through. This same problem occurs with hypo-vigilant clients. Far too often PTSD is ignored as a consideration and they are labeled with Major Depressive Disorder. Can you guess what happens when a client cycles back and forth between hyper and hypo-vigilant states? You guessed it, they are sometimes mislabeled as having Bipolar Disorder. All of these diagnoses may be appropriate if the cause of the issue is not rooted in a traumatic experience.

Anecdotally, during my time as a community mental health professional almost every child I worked with was diagnosed as having Bipolar Disorder.

However, all of these children also had extensive traumatic histories that did not appear to be taken into consideration. The psychiatrist would look at their symptoms and give them medication to try to move them into the window of tolerance. The problem with this methodology is it does not heal the root of the problem. Medications are not effective in treating PTSD, only the symptoms of PTSD. Later in this book we'll talk about evidence-based therapies that work well for people struggling with PTSD.

Our educational system struggles to support children impacted by PTSD. Far too often we view the restlessness, defiance, and aggression of hyper vigilance as something we can punish out of children. Similarly, we see the disconnecting, isolating, shutdown behavior caused by hypo-vigilance as something we need to punish children for. If we could punish our way out of this problem, the problem would have been gone a long time ago. The reality is that students suffering from PTSD struggle to stay in that window of tolerance. This is their body's way of trying to keep them safe in an unsafe world. Punishing and removing these students only reinforces their worldview that they are bad, broken, and people will not help, love, and support them. We've got to get serious about loving and supporting these students to operate within a window of tolerance rather than relying on old practices of punishing them or removing them from school.

Reflection Questions

1. Describe how a person's "window of tolerance" is impacted by trauma?

2. How does your growing understanding of student behaviors impact how you feel about your school discipline procedures?

3. How can we move our focus away from a punishment model into a positive discipline model?

Chapter 11

Neuroplasticity & the Power of Therapeutic Moments

"For years mental health professionals taught people that they could be psychologically healthy without social support, that "unless you love yourself, no one else will love you."...The truth is, you cannot love yourself unless you have been loved and are loved. The capacity to love cannot be built in isolation."
~ *Bruce D. Perry*

After all this difficult information about trauma, I bet you're ready for some good news! Well, here it is. The good news about all this trauma is that our brains are constantly re-wiring themselves, a process called neuroplasticity. The younger you are, the quicker your brain can rewire itself via positive or negative experiences. I'm always surprised by how quickly high school kids can change, how quickly they can heal and grow. And, when we catch it earlier in younger students like Johnny, he will have even more neuroplasticity than high school students.

So, with this biological flexibility on our side, how do we rewire our students' brains? By utilizing something Dr. Bruce Perry calls "therapeutic moments." Essentially, every positive interaction you have with your students creates new neural pathways to the front of the brain. Interestingly, short interactions actually rewire the brain faster than longer ones. So, everytime you smile at your students and tell them you're excited to see them, you provide them with a therapeutic moment. This is why Victor Bell from the earlier Hero Spotlight is so successful as an educator. He is constantly helping to re-wire his students' brains with short positive interactions. Similarly, I consciously make the decision every class period to rewire my student's brains as they walk in the door. They're always met with a kind greeting and I'm checking in to find out what's new with them and ask how they're doing.

Increasing Positive Teacher Interactions

We've talked some about interacting with students when they are in the back of the brain but, how you interact with your students when they are well-regulated in the front of the brain will also have a huge impact on your ability to support them when they are triggered. Below are some of the best strategies I've found to support your students on a daily basis.

10 to 1: This refers to 10 positive interactions for every negative interaction. Most of your students who've experienced significant trauma have not received much positive attention. Adults have not paid much attention unless they do something wrong. It is important to remember that poorly-behaved children are simply sometimes children who would rather be "beaten than ignored." Their difficult upbringing has wired their brains to seek out attention (a primary need) with negative behavior. If we want to rewire our students' brains to seek attention by doing positive things we need to meet the 10:1 ratio to change these patterns of behavior.

You may be thinking, my most difficult students rarely do things right in my class! How am I supposed to get to the 10:1 ratio? I do this by "cheating." To start, I tell them I'm excited to see them as soon as they walk in the door. Then I compliment their shoes or talk with them about an activity they're involved in. I say how proud I am of them, now we have three. I'm constantly looking for creative ways to build my students up to reach that 10:1 ratio. Their 10:1 doesn't need to be based on their classroom behavior. *People are valuable for being people, not just because they behave.* This method is powerful for a multitude of reasons:

1) It builds my relationship with them more quickly. Every positive interaction with me is "money in the bank" I can withdraw when I need to help them cope or challenge improper behavior.

2) It helps increase students' self-worth. Many traumatized students show the world that they're tough and have it all together on the outside but on the inside they are often putting themselves down and have very low self-worth. By consistently building them up in my classroom, they can start to see themselves differently, recognize their strengths, and believe they have value. Typically, when students start to love themselves they'll start to change their self destructive behaviors also.

3) The 10:1 ratio helps rewire their brain to seek out attention with positive behavior. My students know that they can count on me to get their daily intake of positive attention. They show up to class early to tell me the good things they're doing because they know I'll

get excited and praise them for it. I regularly have students in my classroom before school because they desire a positive relationship in their lives. They'll even bring students that are not in my program, because who doesn't like hearing good stuff about themselves?! This is not flattery. This is the necessary process of helping a student re-learn their value when they weren't taught accurately as a child

Remember, the more traumatized your student is, the longer this process will take. Severely traumatized students don't feel safe at school and it will take them longer to feel safe with you. Their brain is working hard to ensure their safety and other people have previously been the most dangerous thing in their world.

Body Language: 80% of communication comes through body language and your body language can help students feel safer or less safe. For example, invading a student's personal space can cause a triggered response. Squaring up your body is more threatening than tilting your body when facing a student. Crossing your arms or legs while talking with a student can make them less likely to feel safe with you. As we discussed earlier, male teachers need to understand that the majority of abuse and violence is perpetrated by men. Students can easily be triggered by size, proximity, or tone of voice. Raising our voices can quickly trigger students. Men's lower frequency voices can remind students of past abuse. As a male teacher I think that there is a huge need for more men in this profession because so many students lack a healthy male role model. Many students will gravitate to you just based on your gender. Even so, we must be aware of the potential triggering nature of simply who we are or how we look or sound.

School Culture: Healing Takes All of Us

This is also why classroom culture is so important. I'm only one person in our school building. My interactions with the students are critical but I'm only one of 20-30 adults. But, what if all of our teachers and students understood the power of "therapeutic moments?" In my classroom, I take the opportunity to teach my students about trauma and about the power of therapeutic moments. We have several discussions about how they can re-wire each other's brains much faster than I ever could through positive, kind, supportive interactions. Even peer-to-peer, they can help each other create positive neural pathways to the front of the brain. By educating them, they learn that when they're kind to each other it has a real impact. The best moments I've seen as a teacher were not because of the interactions I've had with students. The best moments are when students love and support each other.

An example of this ability to heal one another took place during one of my classes. That day, a senior girl talked about a deep emotional wound from her father abandoning her and saying she was always a disappointment to him. From there, a freshman girl became emotional and talked about all she ever wanted was a father. In her case, he showed up when she was seven, making it the happiest day of her life. Then, after a week he left and has never returned. Even in their individual pain, the freshmen girl burst into tears and was comforted by the senior girl. There was so much healing in that moment and those two formed an incredible bond despite their age difference. They supported each other all year, constantly building each other up.

This example was all possible because these students understood and practiced the idea of "therapeutic moments" and the power they have to rewire each other's brains. Students want to matter, they want to be significant, but they often just don't know how. Learning the value of "therapeutic moments" gives them the opportunity to change the lives of their peers. This is the type of classroom culture that allows students to feel safe coming to your room and sharing that a classmate is struggling with a personal issue or that they are struggling themselves. Building a positive classroom culture helps you rewire your students' brains exponentially faster than doing it by yourself.

This concept of overall school culture is of paramount importance. If I'm doing a great job of mentoring, supporting, and caring for my most traumatized students, but the teacher they have next hour is meeting the same students with constant negative interactions, it's going to take longer to have a positive impact. The faster we get our entire staff and district on board, the quicker we can see the lives of students transformed. As an example, when I speak at school districts I encourage them to allow all support staff to attend. Administrative staff, bus drivers, custodians, nurses, and paraprofessionals can have a huge impact on how quickly our students may recover from trauma and thrive.

Conversely, if the rest of the staff is not on board it can be very discouraging. In fact, I've experienced this first hand. I worked in a district that was very un-trauma informed. I worked passionately to support these students and felt like I made an impact. But, I was so discouraged by how these students were treated by other teachers and administration. When I addressed this issue with them I was met with resistance. I knew that if I was going to thrive in education I had to find a school with the same values system as I had. Once I joined the team at the next school I immediately felt like I found my home. Here, everyone was working together to meet the needs of students and they recovered so much quicker than I had seen before in my career. The comparison of those two schools was an eye-opening example of how critical it is to have a trauma-informed school culture.

Hero Spotlight: Nate Brinkley

Nate is a behavior interventionist at an elementary school. Nate is a master of making sure all of his students feel included as a part of the community. He saw a student who felt left out because her family couldn't afford Jordan shoes and he had a great idea. The girl was wearing Chuck Taylors so Nate gave her the history behind Chucks and explained that he also owned a few pairs. He wore those Chucks on Friday and took a picture with that little girl to make sure she felt included. Next thing you knew all the kids wanted to wear Chucks with Nate. Nate made sure all the students who couldn't afford Chucks got a pair. Now, instead of some students feeling left out by their shoes, Nate created an environment where affordable footwear brought all of his students together. He understands the value of one person's ability to help heal another.

Hero Spotlight: Peggy Rodgers

Peggy is what I would call a "Hall of Fame administrative professional." She greets every person who walks through the front door of the school. Her consistent love and kindness to every student who enters the school has touched thousands of lives. I was so happy when she was recognized for her life of service and placed in her school's Hall of Fame. As a community mental health professional I entered so many different schools and how I was greeted at the door could dramatically impact my day. People like Peggy who meet people with kindness day after day create thousands of "therapeutic moments" and touch the lives of many more people than they could ever imagine.

I'm sure if you read this far you're ready to make a bigger impact on the students you work with. In the next section of the book we will learn specific tools you can use as educators to support students impacted by trauma.

Reflection Questions

1. Name two ways you can create more therapeutic moments throughout the day for your students.

2. How can you create a classroom culture where students provide therapeutic moments for each other?

Chapter 12

Counseling & Trauma-Informed Therapy

"Healing from trauma can also mean strength and joy. The goal of healing is not a papering-over of changes in an effort to preserve or present things as normal. It is to acknowledge and wear your new life – warts, wisdom, and all – with courage." ~ Catherine Woodiwiss

As educators we are generally not involved with therapy, but I think it's important for us to have a greater understanding of what treatments are effective for trauma recovery, PTSD, etc. For a long time, people suffering with PTSD were asked to address their symptoms with talk therapy. The potential problem with talk therapy is that when people recall their traumatic events they're often triggered and sent to the back of the brain. Remember, in the back of the brain the only thing to do is fight, flight, or freeze. When approaching trauma in this way, it can be more difficult to process the traumatic events and heal. I've spoken with many trauma survivors who have found that talk therapy made their symptoms worse. This is because trauma and PTSD require a different therapeutic model to ensure that the individual isn't triggered and can stay in the front of the brain where healing can happen.

Cognitive Processing Therapy (CPT) can be an effective treatment for PTSD. This therapy focuses on resolving "stuck points." These "stuck points" are typically ideas in your head that revolve around guilt and shame. CPT helps the client realize that the traumatic event was not your fault and helps clients learn to feel safe in their surroundings. This type of therapy is very effective but can be difficult to locate depending on where you live.

Prolonged Exposure (PE) is a type of therapy where the client will face their triggers over and over again until the brain learns that they are safe. This type of therapy can be effective but has high dropout rates because people don't like the feelings that come from being triggered over and over again.

EMDR (eye movement desensitization reprocessing) is a type of therapy that uses bi-lateral stimulation to help the brain heal from traumatic memories. Admittedly, I was very skeptical of EMDR when I first heard about it, but over 30 studies have shown it to be very effective. It is widely available and I have witnessed so many people recover with this therapy. I recommend it more than any other therapy for trauma-recovery and PTSD.

It is so important that we make sure that we are treating trauma and PTSD with trauma-informed therapists who use evidence-based models for therapy. I've often seen students go to therapy for years with little change in their outcomes, often because they were not receiving evidence-based therapy. All of the therapies above typically last less than ten sessions. If attending weekly, that means that you can be significantly healed from PTSD in two and half months. Help is available but you must know where to look. Keywords to look for are "trauma-informed" as well as certifications in the therapies mentioned above. Students may have access to specific providers through their insurance or, if their family can afford to do so, pay a therapist out of pocket. Thankfully, many schools are recognizing the need to have partnerships with local therapists, group practices, and/or have a clinician on staff for the district.

Additionally, it is appropriate to treat PTSD with medications sometimes, but remember you are only treating the symptoms, not the root cause. People are not healed from PTSD only using medication. To be clear, I'm not anti-medication. Sometimes medication can be a great tool to help bring a person to a place where greater healing can happen. However, we have to make sure to balance medication with the realization that trauma-specific therapy and healing are essential to the process. Far too frequently the root issues of trauma go unnoticed or untreated in our mental health system.

Post-Traumatic Growth

It's imperative that we do not view these traumatized students as "less than." It is extremely hopeful to realize that when we provide these students with the right amount of support they will become stronger, more empathetic, and more resilient. This process is known as "post-traumatic growth."

NORMAL LIFE

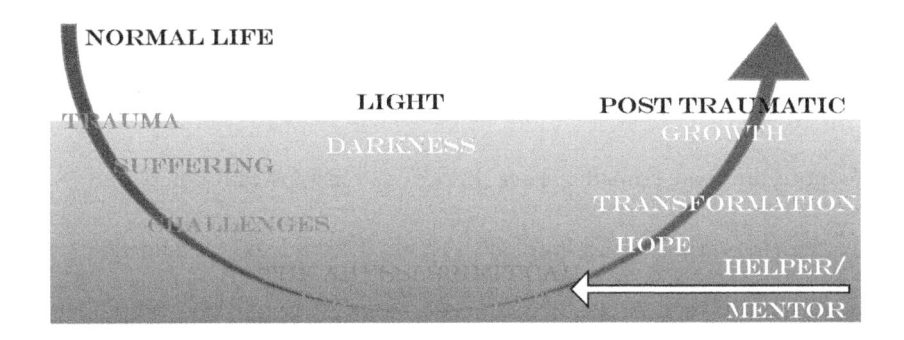

TRAUMA LIGHT POST TRAUMATIC
SUFFERING DARKNESS GROWTH
CHALLENGES TRANSFORMATION
  HOPE
  HELPER/
  MENTOR

Consider the graphic above. Post-traumatic growth is when an individual experiences trauma, suffering, and challenges, finally reaching a point where they need support from others in order to get out. This is where our heroes enter. Heroes provide healthy relationships, love, and support. This helps the person heal and grow. After reflecting upon post-traumatic growth, many people will find that they are actually a stronger, more talented person because of this healing process. Many people have shared with me that they wouldn't wish their trauma away because they know that it was instrumental in them becoming the person they are today.

As another way to help traumatized students, I help them understand this post-traumatic growth process. I encourage them to see how the challenging experiences in their life have given them hidden superpowers.

These superpowers grow out of these challenges. Students become empowered when they realize that they are more independent, appreciate life more, are more empathic, have deeper relationships with others, and have grown personally and spiritually as a result of their post-traumatic growth.

When we help our students heal, experience, and understand post-traumatic growth, they can become some of the most important people in our community. Our schools are full of educators who have experienced post-traumatic growth. Many of us are drawn to the profession because we want to be the hero in someone else's life, the same kind of hero someone was for us.

Reflection Questions

1. How can you increase your understanding and awareness of evidence-based counseling techniques to help people find resources in your community?

2. In your own words, how would you describe post-traumatic growth in a way that can provide hope to a student or their parents?

Chapter 13

Understanding Attachment

"Fire can warm or consume, water can quench or drown, wind can caress or cut. And so it is with human relationships; we can both create and destroy, nurture and terrorize, traumatize and heal each other." ~ Bruce D. Perry

When teachers understand their student's attachment styles and attachment needs, the student's behaviors make much more sense. There are four basic types of attachment. Our attachment style is based on how consistently we had our needs met from birth to three years old. Unfortunately, traumatic events can disrupt and change our attachment. For the purpose of this book we will keep it very simple and focus on how these attachment styles impact your relationships with students.

1) **Secure Attachment:** These students had their needs consistently met as children. Their primary caregiver was predictable, consistent, and trustworthy. As a child they were comfortable exploring, learning, and playing. These students have had their needs met and so they assume that people tend to be good and will treat them well. They are able to

build healthy relationships with others. About 56% of your students will be securely attached. They tend to be a joy to work with. They learn quickly and develop good relationships with their teachers.

2) **Anxious Attachment** (also known as Ambivalent): These students had an inconsistent caregiver. Sometimes their needs were met while other times they were not. This mixed message gives these students a feeling of insecurity. They develop a strong fear of abandonment and have a strong dependency on others. In your classroom these students are constantly looking for your validation. Is this the way you want it? Is this good enough? Your slightest amount of negative feedback can leave them feeling like you don't care about them anymore. This can be very frustrating and challenging as a teacher because it feels like they are constantly reaching for your attention, but that isn't it. They don't want your attention, they want a relationship with you. This is because they're not securely attached and it constantly feels like that relationship is slipping away.

The good news is the more often you can meet their attachment needs the more securely attached they will become in their life and with you. Taking that extra time to assure them that you appreciate them and their work can make all the difference. I once worked with a very anxiously attached student and anytime I would praise another student she would perk up and say, "I did that too." She needed constant validation that I still cared about her.

Thankfully, by understanding that she was anxiously attached, I didn't see her as attention-seeking. Instead, I viewed her behavior as a deep longing for connection. She desperately wanted someone in her life to care about her. I've coached so many football players over the years who are anxiously attached. They want feedback on every rep. I used to get so frustrated with them, but now I understand the root of this behavior and try to give them as much feedback as they need to feel secure. Often, about 20% of your students are anxiously attached.

3) **Avoidant Attachment:** These students had a primary caregiver who was disengaged, distant and unavailable. Their needs of being loved,

seen, and understood were dismissed and ignored. These students were forced to meet their own needs. They tend to be dismissive of their own feelings and the feelings of others. They struggle to make deep connections with others. These students tend to be very independent. They avoid creating deeper relationships with staff and peers. As you develop a closer relationship with them they tend to pull away from you because it feels uncomfortable for them. They are stuck because all people long for connection but, when they start to develop a close relationship it feels very foreign and they have an instinct to resist or sabotage the relationship. These students are very difficult to build relationships with, and it takes a lot of time and patience. By understanding their attachment style you will be less discouraged when they pull away over and over again. By being consistent with them you are helping them become more securely attached over time. Typically, about 23% of your students have avoidant attachment.

4) **Disorganized Attachment:** These students had a primary caregiver who was chaotic and abusive. The caregiver was a source of fear. These students will still attach to their abusive caregiver because all humans

are wired to connect. They are constantly stuck between staying safe and trying to fulfill their needs for connection. They feel helpless and hopeless because no matter what they do they cannot get their needs met. These students spend a great deal of their lives in the back of their brains in fight, flight, or freeze responses. They cycle back and forth between hyper and hypo arousal. These are often your most challenging students. They have no idea how to calm their fear response and don't know how to get their needs met. It takes a great deal of time and energy for them to feel safe enough with you to build a connection. Typically, about 1% of students have disorganized attachment.

By understanding your students' attachment styles you can make great sense of the root of their behaviors and meet them with an empathic response. By consistently meeting your students needs you are also helping them become more securely attached over time. Additionally, if a student you are working with is struggling with insecure attachment, attachment therapy may be very beneficial for them.

Reflection Questions

1. How does understanding your students' attachment styles change the way you view their behaviors?

2. How can you meet your students' attachment needs during the day?

Chapter 14

Social Emotional Skills

"If your emotional abilities aren't in hand, if you don't have self-awareness, if you are not able to manage your distressing emotions, if you can't have empathy and have effective relationships, then no matter how smart you are, you are not going to get very far." ~ Daniel Goleman

Social emotional skills is the term used to describe an individual's ability to regulate thoughts, emotions, and behavior. A student's abilities in this area are strongly tied to the health of their relationships and ability to be successful in school. In fact, social emotional skills are so vital that they can help predict whether a third grader will graduate from college. I'm encouraged by the number of elementary schools adopting social emotional learning programs like Second Step and Character Strong to guide a school-wide effort in this area. Administrators are starting to understand that the students who have deficits in their social emotional skills will continue to struggle in school until we deal with these deficiencies. To that end, we need more middle and high schools to understand the deficits that their students have in their social emotional learning and to adopt more of these programs as well. The remainder of this chapter will focus on the five social emotional skills students need to be successful.

5 Social Emotional Skills Students Need to Be Successful

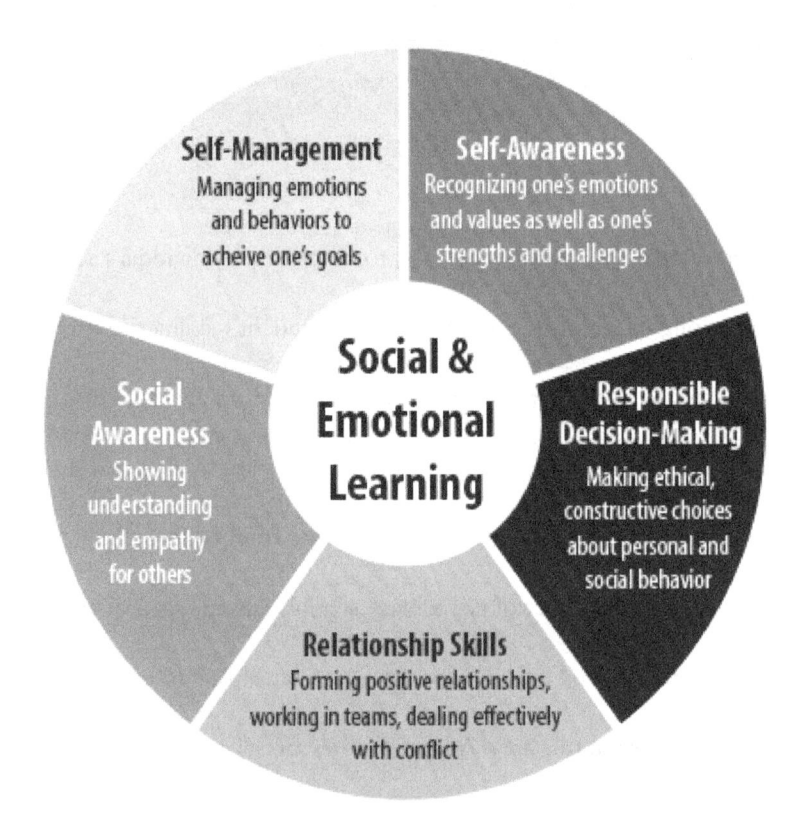

Social & Emotional Learning

- **Self-Management**: Managing emotions and behaviors to acheive one's goals
- **Self-Awareness**: Recognizing one's emotions and values as well as one's strengths and challenges
- **Responsible Decision-Making**: Making ethical, constructive choices about personal and social behavior
- **Relationship Skills**: Forming positive relationships, working in teams, dealing effectively with conflict
- **Social Awareness**: Showing understanding and empathy for others

Self-Awareness: This is the ability to recognize your own emotional state. Boys tend to struggle with this more than girls, particularly older boys. Some young men can't identify if they are angry, anxious, and/or depressed or how these emotions are impacting their behavior. For most of our boys the only safe emotion to express is anger. They might be very depressed or anxious but can only express it as anger because expressing sadness would be viewed as feminine or weak. Even though it is often more challenging with boys, it's important we help all students learn to identify how they are feeling. The more we practice identifying emotional states, the more aware we become of our emotions.

To practice this, I typically start the conversation with something like "you look tense" or "it seems like something is bothering you." These prompts allow the students to explore what's going on inside and give them an opportunity to label these feelings. It is important not to label their feelings for them as preventing them from looking inward can rob them of their story and ability to grown in their emotional intelligence.

Responsible Decision Making: This is the ability to slow down and think before you act. Many of our students struggle with impulse control but it is a skill they can learn with frequent practice by creating a gap between impulse and action. In practice, I use the S.T.O.P. method (Stop, Think,

Observe, Plan) to help them move toward the front of their brain. By stopping, they create space to think about their decision. Next, they think and observe about what the outcomes will be with different decisions. Last, they plan what their best option is. Many of us do this hundreds of times daily without putting any thought to it but our students who struggle with impulse control need help developing this. Like so many things we've discussed, the more they practice this skill the more proficient they will become at decision making.

Relationship Skills: This is the ability to create and maintain positive and healthy relationships. If you grew up in a home where people calmly talked through their problems and resolved them in cooperative ways, then you probably have strong relationships skills. Unfortunately, many of our students grow up in homes where yelling, screaming, and hitting are how conflict is resolved. The primary way we learn relationship skills is from the home environment we grow up in. So many of our students from unhealthy homes can make friends but they don't have the skills to maintain them. This is because once there is some kind of conflict, they don't have the skills necessary to resolve the conflict in a healthy way. These students need guidance on how to work with others, how to deal with conflict, how to create friendships, how to take turns, how to apologize, etc. When we recognize that our students have deficiencies in these areas we can address it and help them practice doing it correctly.

Social Awareness: This is the ability to understand how someone else feels and experience empathy. No matter where I travel to speak, I hear the same thing, "Why are kids so mean to each other these days?" For example, when I was growing up, if I bullied another student I would say something to put them down and I might feel superior in that moment. Some of my peers might laugh. Then, after I had a moment to reflect, I would think about their facial expression and I would understand how I hurt them based on the look on their face. This process of recognition is how our brains are wired for empathy. We understand how another person feels by looking at their facial expressions and equating that to what we've learned and experienced about those expressions.

However, one of our challenges today is that many of our interactions are happening virtually. Students are still bullying but, when it is done digitally via text or social media, they are not getting the facial feedback that helps develop an empathic response. As trauma-informed educators, we know cell phones are not going anywhere, so we need to get serious about teaching empathy to our students. This will require hundreds of intentional conversations where we talk about how the other person feels. As a quick example, when a student expresses a teacher isn't being "fair", it gives me a great opportunity to explain the teacher's point of view and how the student's behavior also makes the teacher feel. Through repetitive conversations like this about friends, family, and teachers, students can begin to understand how other people feel about their behavior and vice versa. These types of conversations are what helps wire their brain for empathy.

Self Management: This is the ability to regulate your own emotional state with healthy coping skills. For example, if I'm feeling angry, maybe I'll go for a run. If I'm feeling sad I'll listen to music. If I'm anxious I'll use lavender essential oil for calm. Just like I have my own strategies to cope with regular stressors, every student needs a plan to manage their own mental health. But, because no one plan works for everyone, I help my students create a plan of coping skills that work for them. I also help them figure out what situations they struggle with the most and help them develop plans to manage those specific situations. The more students practice and see success with positive coping skills the more likely they are to use them throughout their lives. Remember, if we don't teach health coping skills to our students we shouldn't be surprised when they start using unhealthy ones. In the coming chapters we will talk about more coping skills and student success plans to help achieve these very things.

Hero Spotlight: Kim Korman

I coached college football for about a decade after getting my Masters Degree in Counseling. When we decided that making the shift out of coaching college football was the best move for my family, Kim Korman was the one who gave me a shot as a community-based mental health professional at the Arthur Center where she serves as the supervisor of youth services. Even with a degree in counseling, I had spent so long coaching football I was intimated by the challenge of this new job.

One of the very first kids I got on my caseload was a 10-year-old boy with a huge file who had already been in a residential treatment facility for almost a year. The contents of his file showed he had some very extreme and dangerous behaviors. Feeling insecure, I went to Kim and said "How can I possibly help this kid? I have no idea where to even start." She responded, "Just connect and build a relationship with him." It sounded so simple and I remember feeling relieved. I can do that, I thought to myself. After a two-hour drive to St Louis, they let me in the locked doors to see this little boy. Despite what his file made him out to be, he wasn't a monster at all. We played Jenga for over an hour and I learned about his life and his dreams. He was really good at Jenga too, he beat me several times. Year after year, I got to see this kid improve and, eventually, move back home and live a regular life. None of this would have been possible without Kim's wise advice of putting relationships first and giving this football coach a chance to work with these kids. While this is just one example of one kid, I share it to give you hope that the simple act of building a relationship is not only a great place to start, but more effective than you may realize.

Reflection Questions

1. Which of the five categories of social-emotional learning feels strongest for you? How can you use this to help students?

2. Tell one of your favorite stories of building a relationship with a student and how that helped him or her.

Chapter 15

Distressed Students & the 3 R's

"What we don't need in the midst of struggle is shame for being human."
~ Brené Brown

As we continue to discuss practical application strategies, let's consider some common questions for the classroom. What do you do when a student is upset? What do you do when they are yelling or completely shut down? You may be surprised to learn that the best strategies often start with yourself, not the student. The first thing I always ask myself is, "Are they in the front or the back of the brain?" Of course, when a student is elevated, the answer is always that they are in the back of the brain. But, this thought process is more for me as it helps me stay calm and remind myself that the root of the problem is that they are in the back of the brain in a fight, flight, or freeze response. As we've said already, *they are having a hard time rather than giving me a hard time.*

Next, I remind myself that "calm creates calm" and "chaos creates chaos." I have very little chance to regulate a student if I get upset. Taking a deep breath and remembering that other students will mirror me helps me manage my response. If I stay calm, other students will feel safer and be less likely to be triggered by the student who is upset. When the struggling student is in the back of their brain they cannot understand consequences, process why they are upset, or make plans to change their behavior. In fact, students can only process about 15 words when they are triggered. Instead, all they can do is fight, flight, or freeze. Many educators try to threaten students with severe consequences or talk through complex details of the situation when they are in the back of the brain. This is often counterproductive because it further entrenches the fight, flight, or freeze response.

The 3 R's

The first and most important thing we want to do with a triggered student is help them calm down. A mnemonic to help remember this three-step process of calm is "RELAX, RECONNECT, and RE-TEACH." Remember, your students need safety then connection, only then can they learn. During relax, reconnect, re-teach we are trying to prepare the students brain to be in a position where they can learn from this experience. Each of these R's has a specific strategy: RELAX (safety), RECONNECT (connection), and RE-TEACH (learning). The number one mistake we make in managing student behavior is assuming that all students are in the front of their brains when dealing with discipline. In fact, many are in the back of the brain and not ready to make good choices and receive the information we are giving them. This part of what contributes to students making the same mistakes over and over again.

To explore this further, we will first address the fight, flight, or freeze response with the RELAX step. As mentioned, the first thing you need to do is manage your own emotional response. You have little chance to calm a student if you are escalated by their behavior. You may not be able to control their behavior, but you can control your own response which, in turn, gives them the best opportunity to be successful. Next, we attempt to calm the student by employing a coping strategy. Contrary to popular belief, I've found that when a student is very dysregulated, talking can escalate them inside of calming them down. Talking about the situation that got them triggered often leads to a more dysregulated student.

My most popular "non-talking" coping strategy was using scratch art. Scratch art pads are basically large lottery tickets upon which I ask the student to create a new piece of artwork or simply scratch the entire card off. The student doesn't realize this but by scratching, they are practicing mindfulness. They are focused on this small art project instead of the situation that made them so upset. I've found coloring books to be very effective for the same reason. With elementary kids I use crayons and with high school students I use fine tip sharpies on adult coloring books. The effect is the same. They focus on coloring instead of the triggering situation and the fight, flight, or freeze response starts to dissipate and the front of the brain can reengage. Other tools I've used during the RELAX step are movement (walking, basketball, punching bag, etc.) silence, singing bowls, and breathing exercises. Every student is different so you need to play around with different coping strategies until you find one that works for each student. These specific tools are detailed in coming chapters.

Once we've deescalated the fight, flight, or freeze response, we move onto the RECONNECT step. Often, in the mind of the student, the triggered behavior has damaged the relationship. They feel (sometimes subconsciously) that those school relationships have vanished because they are in trouble. Because of this fear, we need to reconnect with that student before we address the problem behavior, connecting before we correct. I've found the best way to reconnect to a student is to listen to them and validate their experience. You probably feel close to people who listen to your experiences without judgment and your students are no different. The most common mistake I see educators make during this step is that they listen until they hear something they don't agree with and then they interject. It's important to listen to their story without interrupting.

Part of the reason for this extended listening is that trauma impacts how memories are stored and recalled in the brain. Sometimes, when a student is telling you an inaccurate story, they are sharing how they perceived the event. As frustrating as this can sometimes be, this is valuable information for you. While I never validate the poor behavior, I validate the feeling behind it. So, if a student cussed out their teacher I never say it was ok to swear at the teacher. However, I say you must have been very frustrated, angry, anxious, etc. When we respond in this way the student feels heard and it helps build the type of connection we need to support that student. Don't worry, we are not just forgetting the problem behavior. We will address it in the RE-TEACH step.

After the relax and reconnect steps, you hopefully now have a student who is well-regulated and connected with a brain that is in a position to learn. Now we can address the problem behavior. During the final RE-TEACH step, I start by talking to the student about what happened before the behavior. I try to help them find a trigger for the dysregulation and recognize what their body felt like before they lost control. For many students, they feel tense, hot, or have a headache before they lose control. This is their early warning system. Their body is telling them they need to do something before they lose control. Once they're triggered it's too late, so I help them learn to recognize how their body feels before they lose control so they can use this moment to ask for help.

As an example, I once had a 6th grade student who would become very aggressive when he was angry. He destroyed school property and even knocked holes in office walls. The big breakthrough our team had with this student is when he identified that his body gets hot before he loses control. His plan was when he starts feeling hot he leaves class right away and comes straight to my office. From there, we would go through relax, reconnect, re-teach. We were able to teach him to regulate before the explosion.

An additional strategy is to talk with students about supports that they have available in the school setting. We identify a support person(s) they feel comfortable with and make a plan of how they can access them when needed. Lastly, we address the problem behavior. I talk with them about how their behavior impacts other people. I make sure they understand how their behavior made students, teachers, administration, etc. feel.

One Additional "R"

A final step is to talk about how they are going to repair the harm. How are they going to fix what they've broken? Remember, people don't learn by being removed, that's why our criminal justice system is so ineffective in reducing recidivism of crime. People learn by fixing what they broke and developing empathy. For an elementary-aged student, this might look like putting all the books back on the shelf that they knocked down when they were dysregulated. Most of the time at the secondary level, repairing the harm is about fixing damaged relationships. I never force a student to apologize but if this process is done properly the student should recognize how they hurt someone and be in a place where they want to repair that relationship. I always check with the person that they've hurt to make sure they're ready to receive that healing circle of interaction. The last thing you want to do is to force this process before everyone is ready. I've had teachers tell me they're still upset and are not ready to hear an apology from a student yet. That's ok, having everyone emotionally ready for this process is important.

After all this stepwise information you may be thinking, gosh, this trauma-informed process sure sounds like it takes a long time! You're right. Sometimes it does, but it's worth it. Sometimes RELAX, RECONNECT, and RE-TEACH takes an hour and can be done by a teacher during class. Other times it can take several days and a counselor and administrator need to be involved. Every student and situation is unique. But, this 3-step process needs to be used to ensure our students are in the best emotional space possible to learn from their experience.

Hero Spotlight: Kenya Thompson

Mrs. Thompson is a superintendent. It's important that as readers, you all know that I'm not perfect and I don't handle every situation perfectly. At this particular school, when I was coaching high school football I worked with a student who had a very challenging life. He experienced a very traumatic childhood, but he was full of energy and love. He quickly made a home in our school environment and excelled from all the support he received. During a heated playoff football game I was yelling at him from the sidelines to make an adjustment. This caused this young man to be triggered to the back of the brain and he had a melt down on the sideline. Mrs. Thompson met with me the following Monday to talk about the incident.

Thankfully, she never came at me with a "got ya" mentality. Instead, she let me know that she was there to support me but the situation could have been handled better. We talked about my own competitive nature and how it got the best of me in that moment. We discussed the best way to move forward with that student. I was able to apologize to this young man and he was quick to forgive. Having proper support from your administration is so important as our brains work just like our students and we can find ourselves in some difficult, triggering situations ourselves. I never felt attacked during this difficult conversation but Mrs. Thompson also made sure that she was meeting the needs of her students first. This is a difficult line to walk but that's what makes her a great leader. She can have difficult conversations while also making you feel supported.

Reflection Questions

1. How can we ensure that Relax, Reconnect, and Re-teach is happening before we give discipline in our schools?

2. Which of the specific strategies mentioned feel like something you could start implementing today?

3. You read about a time when I struggled to communicate with a student in a healthy way. Talk about a time when you struggled and/or a time when a supervisor met you in kindness as mine did.

Chapter 16

Self-Regulation & Personal Reflection

"People start to heal the moment they feel heard." ~ Cheryl Richardson

The best way to handle our students' dysregulation is to first recognize how it makes us feel as educators. Frequently, when a student is dysregulated that makes the teacher feel uncomfortable to be in a space with the dysregulated student. It can make us feel anxious, angry, or annoyed by the students inability to feel calm in that moment. Our students can feel our dysregulation and, in turn, it makes it much more difficult for them to relax. We need to learn to recognize these feelings and to sit in this discomfort.

Additionally, one of the hardest things about being a parent or educator is that being around children can easily trigger our own childhood traumas. Understanding how our own traumatic experiences are still impacting us today is essential in being the best educator we can be.

To begin this process, we need to understand what is the best version of ourselves at work. How does our body feel, what is the tone of our voice, what do our actions look like? Once we identify the best version of ourselves we can start to notice when we are being triggered by our students.

Interacting with our students can subconsciously trigger our own painful childhood memories. These traumatic events were too painful in the moment for our younger selves to process so we hide them away to prevent being overwhelmed by the amount of pain they created. Our minds work relentlessly to keep us from having to experience these painful memories again, protecting us in two different ways: Via behaviors and unhealthy coping strategies.

When our past trauma gets triggered by a student's behavior, educators can unconsciously begin to exhibit behaviors to help them feel safe in the moment. Some examples of this are educators who get angry as a way to dominate over the student. Others become very controlling because the control helps them feel safe. Some educators try to plan every single possible interaction and have a plan for every scenario because then they feel prepared for the worst. Others simply shut down, ignore, and don't engage.

In addition to these coping behaviors, sometimes we can recognize when our bodies don't feel safe at school. Your body might feel tight, tense, hot, or have headaches or stomach issues. These are all ways your body may be communicating to you that you are being triggered at school. Having a supportive school culture is very important in dealing with triggered educators. To be clear, it is likely we will all be triggered at some point when working in education. Because this happens to all of us, it's not about catching the person doing it "wrong." Instead, it's about noticing that they are struggling to stay regulated and supporting that staff member in working through the issue.

When we are unable to control our students' behavior with the above unhealthy strategies these students may then further trigger us at work. Being a teacher is difficult and many educators deal with these powerful feelings by coping in unhealthy ways. Overeating, drinking, drugs, and risky behavior are not only for traumatized students. They are also all ways that educators sometimes deal with the powerful feelings that come with being triggered at work. It's essential that we become aware of our triggers at school so we become better at recognizing when our colleagues are struggling and get creative in ways to support them during their difficult times.

Reflection Questions

1. How can educators support one another when we become dysregulated during the school day?

2. What is one way you can help yourself return to feeling regulated during a tough day at school?

Chapter 17

Building Relationships: Quality or Quantity?

"The more healthy relationships a child has, the more likely he will be to recover from trauma and thrive. Relationships are the agents of change and the most powerful therapy is human love." ~ Bruce D. Perry

We've learned that healthy relationships are the key to healing from trauma, but how do we build relationships with students? Some educators are natural relationship builders, "kid magnets", and this part comes easy. However, some educators struggle building relationships with lots of students and may connect well with a specific few or type. It's important to remember the students in your community need both kinds of teachers. Remember, every teacher in your building is uniquely qualified to connect with a student in your building. It's not about the number of students you reach, it's about the quality of the connection.

I've seen librarians and art teachers play pivotal roles in being a safe place for students to congregate and connect. While I try my hardest to connect with every student, I'm not going to be the best fit for every kid. Maybe the

English teacher or the tennis coach is the perfect fit or maybe it's a custodian. That's why it's so important that we get everyone on board with the trauma-informed care movement. Our next hero spotlight is an example of one of these unexpected connections.

Hero Spotlight: Park County School District #1 Transportation Staff

I got the opportunity to provide trauma-informed training to the staff at Park County School District #1 in Powell, Wyoming. When I work with an entire district I encourage them to have all staff present at the training. Bus drivers, custodians, food service personnel, and paraprofessionals all provide therapeutic moments for our students. Due to a scheduling conflict the transportation staff was unable to attend the training. But, the administration understood how impactful these people are to their students and brought me back to just train the transportation staff.

As my presentation is very interactive, I was concerned that the bus drivers wouldn't participate as openly as the teachers typically do. Boy, was I wrong. They were my favorite group I've ever worked with. They were so passionate about how they could support students impacted by trauma in their role. They knew that they had the potential to be the first and last therapeutic moment for so many students. They also see these kids' homes everyday and are often the first ones to notice when a family is struggling and may need extra support. I learned so much from the transportation staff at PCSD #1.

Hero Spotlight: Lisa Haglund

Lisa Haglund is a school social worker. Lisa is incredible at recognizing the needs of a family and helping connect them to the community resources that they need. Lisa and I were asked to visit a new family in our school district due to poor attendance. When we arrived at the home we realized that the family of six was living in a camper. We approached the mother and she was so worried that we were there to take away her kids. She explained that her husband had lost his job and they were evicted. Lisa quickly calmed her worries and explained that we were here to help her through this difficult time. Lisa helped her make a list of resources that she needed to get through this challenging transition. The mother's demeanor quickly changed and she was overwhelmed with tears when she realized that we were there to help and support her instead of making her situation more challenging. Not only is Lisa helping these families but she is building strong ties between families and our schools by providing these supports.

No matter what kind of teacher you are, I've used the below formula for years to connect with challenging students:

1) **Build Rapport**: The first thing we want to do with students is to build a relationship with them. We want to be viewed as "their teacher," the person that they can go to and count on in the building. We do this by getting interested in what they are interested in. Talk to them about something they love talking about. I had a student once that was really into LARPING. I had no idea what larping was. He talks endlessly about how it stands for live action role play, and how they dressed up as different characters and had foam swords and bean bags for magic. Now, I don't do a lot of larping on the weekends, but I kept asking him questions about it because I knew it would help me build a relationship with him.

The number one mistake I see teachers make when starting to build a rapport is to start with what the teacher wants from them. The teacher will only talk about how they want this assignment done and this behavior in their class. That's not how you build a relationship in real life and that's not how you build one with students. Play the long game, understand that we get these kids for a long time, start with relationship building and the rest of the year will be so much easier. Don't forget to smile! Your smile is your greatest asset. Lastly, be consistent. Not many people in these students' lives have been consistent. Todd Wittaker once said at a professional development session I attended, "The hardest part of being a teacher is that it matters everyday." Those words struck a chord with me. We need to be there for our students on our good days and more importantly on our bad days.

2) **Raise Self-Worth**: The next step is to raise your students self-worth. How many of you have all of your retirement income invested in Blockbuster Video? Why don't you? Because the stock is worthless. Traumatized students feel like Blockbuster Video. They are not going to invest in themselves until they start seeing themselves in a more

positive light. This is where the 10:1 ratio comes in handy. By consistently giving them positive feedback they will start to see themselves the way you see them. Find little things that they do well and get really excited about it. I've seen so many students dramatically alter their behavior once they started to believe in themselves and that they could actually be successful in life.

As a full disclosure, I was that student. I didn't think that I could be successful in anything until I started having success on the football field. Being good at something was huge for my self-worth. The attention I got for being successful was essential in me believing in myself. Before long, I was doing much better academically. I was acting out less in class just because I thought that I could do something positive with my life and that my education was going to be crucial in obtaining that success. So many of these traumatized students act like they have it all together and have an inflated sense of self, but this is generally just a facade that they put on that hides that they really feel poorly about themselves. Once you get these kids feeling like "Netflix stock" you'll be amazed how much they engage in classes they don't even like.

3) **Smart Goals**: After we've built a strong rapport and have students starting to believe in themselves, the next step is to start making goals. I'm a big believer in SMART goals because it teaches students how doing things they don't like today (like algebra) can help them create the life they want down the road.

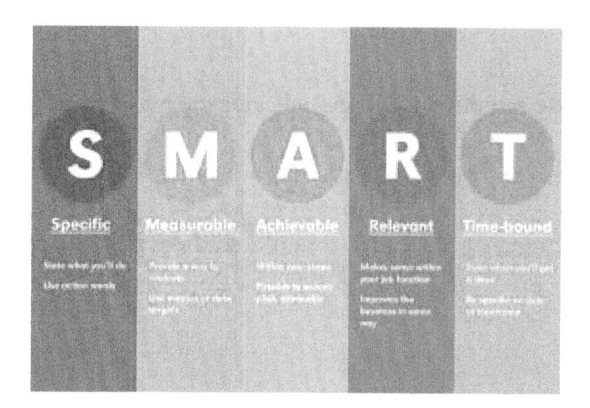

In a personal example, I had a student who was at high risk for dropping out and not graduating. He constantly talked about gaming and esports. His goal was to be an esports athlete in college. Now, at the time I didn't really believe that you could go to college for esports, but I didn't want to squash his goal. Instead, we talked about how he needed to graduate high school in order to go to college for esports, and how he needed to pass English to graduate from high school. We developed a measurable goal that I could hold him accountable for to get his English grade to passing. Everytime we met we would talk about his dream of playing esports in college and how today he needed to work on his English assignments to make that dream a reality. Fast forward a year and a half later, he was graduating and accepting a $30,000 annual scholarship to play e-sports. These students have a hard time understanding how their behavior today will impact them down the road. They can't see past today, so it's our job to help break those steps into manageable chunks and hold them accountable for working towards their dream.

4) **Maintain Progress**: Have you ever tried to lose weight before? Did you lose one pound a week until you disappeared? Of course not, that's because change doesn't happen in a linear fashion. Our students are no different. They will make tremendous progress and then backslide.

Most of the time the backslide is caused by things that are out of our control and/or the student's control. That's okay. That's part of the process. That's how growth works. It's our job as educators to be there for them when they regress and to get them back on track as quickly as possible. I've seen way too many educators give up on a student during the regression but, this is when they need you the most. I always expect my students to regress around the holidays, summer break, and when the weather gets nice. This is part of the process, be ready for it.

Reflection Questions

1. What stage are you at in the relationship building process with your most challenging student?

2. How can you make sure you are not skipping steps while relationship building?

Chapter 18

Student Support Plans

"If you have suffered from trauma, one of the most healing things that can happen to you is being seen. Being seen doesn't have to mean that someone actually lays their eyes on you, although that certainly helps." ~ Timothy Morton

Every student struggling at your school needs their own trauma-informed care plan. This plan is important for a multitude of reasons. First, it will help you share information between team members. By utilizing all the information, the team can serve students better. Second, it helps focus on students' strengths first. Far too often we become deficit-focused with these students. We need to switch to being strengths-based and focus on all the amazing gifts these students have. Third, it helps us connect with students faster.

Of course, one of the biggest challenges working with students impacted by trauma is they can be difficult to engage. A student support plan allows team members to understand their students better and more efficiently build relationships with them. To develop an effective student support plan, consider the following:

1) **Strengths**: What are this student's talents? Where do they excel? What makes them special and unique? Students who have been traumatized are not less than other students. They have gained amazing super powers from their most challenging moments. It's our job to find these strengths and to use them and celebrate them as much as possible.

2) **Interests and Expertise**: What interests do they have? What do they spend their free time doing? What expertise do they have? If we can figure out what our students are interested in, this can help us connect to students who are difficult to build relationships with.

As an example, I had a student who was wrecking my lesson plans at the start of the year. He was so disrespectful and disruptive. I tried to connect to him, tried to explain to him how his behavior had impacted me and the class, but it didn't change anything. I started to think that maybe my program and class would be better if he wasn't in it. I had to think about the greater good right? As I thought about removing him I started to think about the fact that my program was the last opportunity for him to be successful in this school. If I kicked him out, who would be able to support him, who would help him?

So, I went back to the drawing board and tried to connect with him again. We ended up connecting over Star Trek. I don't know much about Star Trek, but I knew just enough about Spock and Captain Kirk to keep the conversation moving. After a few days of talking about Star Trek before and after class he started to show up to my class to hang out before school. Soon after that, the negative behaviors dissipated. How great would it have been to have gotten a plan before he showed up to know that he was an expert with all things Star Trek? Star Trek was the answer to unlocking the walls he built up around himself. Every kid has a Star Trek. Every kid has something they are interested in.

3) **Triggers**: It is important for school staff to work together to figure out what is triggering students. The more eyes we have looking for these important details the quicker we can figure out what these triggers are

and ultimately support our students. How often have you had a student with an important anniversary, like the death of a parent, and you had no idea? We miss so many of these obvious triggers because we don't communicate this information effectively between teachers and schools. Imagine getting a new student in your class, but you already know what his strengths, interests, triggers, and coping skills were? All the important work that the teachers before you completed will give you a huge advantage in working with this student.

4) **Coping plan**: What coping skills work for this student? What have you tried that was not effective? How amazing would it be to know this student responds really well when they're given an opportunity to get a drink of water, or five minutes to play with playdoh? Granted, developing coping skills for students is a lot of trial and error. What works for one student will be ineffective for another. But, I also know as a teacher I don't want to have to start over with every new student. Wouldn't it be great to already have a great foundation to understand what this student needs and what works for them?

I encourage all schools to form a Student Support Team to create these plans. This team should have counselors, administration, and teachers. If possible, the team should meet weekly to talk about what is working and what changes need to be made to support these students.

Hero Spotlight: Beth Houf

Beth is a high school principal. But, long before Beth was a best-selling author and National Secondary Principal of the Year she was also an elementary school principal. This was also before I started my trauma-informed journey. We met when I was a community mental health provider and worked with a severely traumatized little girl. Her behaviors were a constant disruption to the school environment. Beth was the first educator I encountered who had the "we'll make it work no matter what mentality."

The staff at this school got creative and created a little space in the room that the girl could retreat to in order to feel safe. Most importantly, Beth and her staff met this little girl with unconditional love everyday. Many educators like Beth have been using trauma-informed care practices before they even knew what trauma-informed care was. They just knew that connecting and loving students worked. This little girl was able to grow and heal because of the kindness she was met with at Beth's school. It doesn't surprise me that Beth has had so much success and accolades in education because she always had the mentality that she would find a way for each kid to be successful in her school.

"Students who are loved at home come to school to learn. Students who aren't come to school to be loved." ~ Nicholas A. Ferroni

Reflection Questions

1. Are the student support plans at your school adequately strengths-based?

2. Depending on your school size, types of staff, etc. who is important to have on your student support team?

Chapter 19

Classroom Tools

"Even the simplest tools can empower people to do great things." ~ Unknown

This is a practical chapter that explores classroom tools that can help regulate your students (and you!). Many of these tools are incredibly simple yet amazingly effective as the easiest and most productive tools I've found.

1) **Adult Coloring Books** (or just coloring books): I find this to be the best strategy I've used as a classroom teacher. The small shapes on the page combined with a fine tipped marker force the student to focus on this task. This act of mindfulness helps clear the mind and focus it on the present. Almost all students love to color and most students are impacted in a positive way. I've also used dot-to-dots as an effective mindfulness strategy. Bonus points for finding coloring books with inspiring messages, more bonus points for hanging the student art all over your room. This is a reminder that you value your students and they can overcome these big emotions.

2) **Guided Meditations**: I start every class period with some sort of guided meditation for five minutes. I've found that several of my students come into class everyday dysregulated. By taking five minutes to practice mindfulness, I can help these students get back to the front of their brains where they can learn. YouTube has hundreds of these guided meditations. (Pro tip: Do not require your students to close their eyes. For some students this is a trigger and will prevent them from relaxing and feeling safe.)

Of course, at first your students may laugh at this idea so I allow them to do whatever they want as long as they don't disturb others. You'll find that quickly they learn to enjoy a few moments of peace in their chaotic lives. Not only am I helping them reach the front of the brain where they can learn in my class but I'm also helping the other teachers they have, because students will be more regulated overall. I'll substitute mindful walks on good weather days, asking the students to feel the warmth of the sun on their skin and to be mindful of the way the breeze feels on their face. My students quickly began to look forward to these peaceful moments and will quickly remind me when I would forget our mindfulness time and jump right into a lesson. As a teacher you will also benefit greatly from these moments of peace. I've found that by practicing mindfulness five times each day I'm much calmer and more effective when I see challenging behavior from my students.

3) **Essential Oils**: The quickest way to the brain is through the nose. Lavender works really well to calm down hyper-aroused students. I've also found that lavender works well for students who struggle with anxiety. I've had football players I've coached ask me for lavender on game day because they were nervous about the big game.

Cinnamon is very effective in invigorating hypo-aroused students. These students need help getting energized and cinnamon can help achieve that relatively quickly. Diffusers work well if you want your entire classroom or office to have these benefits. Make sure you check with your local schools rules on this because some schools do not allow it. Students can wear necklaces or bracelets designed for essential oils, this can be a great way for them to give themselves a dose of coping during the day as needed.

4) **How Drake are you Feeling?**: This likert scale can be very effective in getting students to talk about their emotional state. Asking a high school boy how they're feeling can lead to short, closed-ended statements like "I'm fine." But, when we ask them a question with a pop-culture reference, "How Drake are you feeling?" it can peak their interest and give them an opportunity to think about how they feel and what caused them to feel that way. You can create your own likert scales with SpongeBob, Cardi B, or anything else your student's are interested in. This is a great opportunity to build social-emotional skills.

5) **Calm Safe Spaces**: You can create spaces in your classroom where students can go to cope wherever they are triggered. Rocking chairs are

very effective because their rhythm reduces the stress response. This area could have coloring books, playdoh, headphones for music, or a small trampoline. When you are able to calm your student down in the classroom without removing them, you are building a closer relationship with them and they feel they belong in your class. Everytime we remove students from the classroom we are sending them a message that they do not belong. When students see their peers coping with a stress response, they are learning that dysregulation is a normal part of life, and that we can all regulate our stress response with effective coping skills.

6) **Bio Dots**: I love bio dots. These little pieces of plastic stick to your hand and measure body temperature. If you are old enough to remember mood rings, it's based on the same idea. When people become stressed, their bodies view this as a threat and circulate less blood into the extremities and more blood into the core. This is an automatic survival response. The more stressed you are, the less blood will circulate in your hands and the colder your hands will get. Bio dots measure these temperature changes and change colors to reflect this

change. Some students are very unaware of their emotional state and bio dots can give them the opportunity to reflect on what they're actually feeling.

As an example, if I see a high school boy who is obviously angry I'll ask him, "What's wrong?" and he may blow me off by saying "I'm fine." But, if I ask him if I can put a bio dot on his hand? Then he's hooked. I've never had a student turn down a bio dot and of course he's curious and says "Yes." The dot quickly turns black and I can show him the chart and explain that it says that black means you're stressed. Typically, this will finally get the conversation going. The student will often explain what's going on with their life and why they are stressed all the time. Next, I'll ask the students to try a coping skill to see if we can change the color of the bio dot from black to green. I know if you ask the average high school boy to do deep breathing exercises they'll look at you like you have lobster coming out of your ears. But, if they have a bio dot on their hand all of the sudden they're playing a game. You may be surprised how open they are to trying new coping skills.

7) **Deep Belly Breathing**: This works better than anything else at calming our stress response. This is because our diaphragm rubs against the vagus nerve and calms its signal telling the body to release stress hormones like adrenaline and cortisol. You can teach your students to take deep breaths and watch bio dots change colors. Eventually it will turn green and that student will feel like they accomplished their challenge. This process is so powerful because the student learns to identify their feelings, how to use a coping skill, and learns that the coping skill works because the bio dot changed colors. The students will leave your class with the knowledge they can control how they feel. This simple exercise is empowering because many students feel like they have no control over their life, but when they learn to control their stress response they regain control over their minds and behaviors.

8) **Singing Bowls**: My high school students love singing bowls. Singing bowls are small brass bowls that make sound when you rub them with a small piece of wood. We often use it as part of our mindfulness practices at the beginning of class. Singing bowls are fantastic for mindfulness for all ages because they make a wonderful sound and you

can feel the vibration in your hand. It's an increasingly satisfying coping strategy as they learn to make the sound they want through time and patience.

9) **Pinwheels/Bubbles**: These are great strategies for younger students to work on their breathing. Some students will be resistant to breathing exercises but most of them love a pinwheel or playing with bubbles which activates deep breathing.

10) **Rocking Chairs/Swinging**: Rhythmic motions soothe and heal the brain from trauma. It's no wonder that people of all ages love the rhythmic motion of a rocking chair or a swing. Rocking chairs are easy to add to any classroom and work for all age groups.

11) **Art**: Art can be a great way for students to express what's going on in their lives. Ask your students to draw or paint what's stressing them out. Ask them to make a picture of their family or their home. You can tell a lot about how a student feels about their family by the art they create.

12) **Social Skills Groups**: Very often we have groups of students who have deficiencies in the same area with their social emotional skills. Creating groups to work on these skills can help students learn that they're not alone while also creating environments where they can support each other.

13) **Reward with Extra Time**: We know these students want to connect with us. Rewarding them by eating lunch with them or playing a game with them can make their week.

14) **Before and After School**: These times are underutilized in many schools. Use these times to connect with your students. Give them fun activities they can do in your room. The more time we have with these students the larger the impact will be.

15) **Balloons**: Balloons can be a great visual of our emotional state. We can teach students that a full balloon will soon pop if it doesn't get an opportunity to release the air. Our emotions work the same way. If we

don't release them with coping skills eventually they'll explode out in a way that we don't intend or want them to.

16) **<u>Bring Their Thoughts into their Consciousness</u>:** I frequently ask my students to reflect on the voice in their head. What is that voice saying? Is it kind? Is it supportive? Frequently, students will explain that the voice is their biggest critic. I ask my students to take those comments and ask, "Would you say this to a friend?" If the answer is no then we need to work it out of their head, too. The first step is to notice the voice. The next step is to deny its truth. The last step is to replace it with encouraging commentary.

17) **<u>Pets/Animals</u>:** Animals can be tremendously helpful to trauma survivors. When people don't feel safe around other people, dogs and horses can be instrumental in providing a safe, healthy interaction. One school where I worked had a therapy dog in every building. Whenever I got "stuck" with a kid I brought the dog in and it worked every time. They didn't feel safe with me but they felt safe with that animal. You can also use time with these dogs as a reward mechanism. I've worked

in courtrooms where therapy dogs have been instrumental in helping kids feel safe enough to testify against family members who abused them. I've also witnessed therapy dogs and horses do amazing work with students. Check your school policy on therapy animals.

Healing Trauma Physically

Trauma is often a very physical experience. So, the more we can integrate complex movement and rhythmic movement into our school days the healthier our students will become. One of my pet peeves is when we take recess and physical education away from students. There have been so many studies that have found that giving our students opportunities to move decreases negative behaviors and increases academic outcomes.

Rhythmic movements help heal our brains from traumatic experiences. That's a big reason why many students are drawn to sports where they get opportunities to practice rhythmic movements that help bring them into regulation. Rhythmic movements can be as simple as jumping rope, playing drums, or swinging a golf club. The best evidence-based rhythmic activity for healing from trauma is fly fishing. I walk around a lake everyday after school as a part of my self-care plan. I frequently see Veterans wearing their hats denoting which war they served in while fly fishing. These Veterans likely didn't get prescriptions to treat their PTSD with fly fishing. They've just learned over time that fly fishing helps them feel better. This is true for many of our students, they don't know why they're drawn to these activities but these activities can make a huge difference in helping them become more well regulated.

Complex movement has also been shown to help students become more well-regulated after experiencing trauma. Yoga has been shown to be effective in helping students learn to become more well-regulated. I started a Yoga Club at my school. Yoga teachers tend to be incredible people and I found it easy to find someone who was willing to donate their time to support our students.

As educators we need to be intentional about providing these opportunities for our students. Give them opportunities during the school day for rhythmic and complex movement. It's also important to get these students plugged into after school activities where they will get an opportunity to practice these movements over and over again. It doesn't matter if it's a club, sport, or band. These movements will help your students heal and the relationships they create will also speed up their recovery. That's why the most impactful teachers in your building are often involved with their students after school.

Hero Spotlight: Amy Lee

Amy Lee is a local yoga instructor who volunteered to donate her time to start a Yoga Club. This Yoga Club was especially beneficial for our young women. The club taught them to learn relaxation techniques and to learn how to love their bodies. I frequently saw teachers join in on these sessions as part of their self-care plans. Who is the Amy Lee in your community?

Reflection Questions

1. Name two of the suggested tools you could begin implementing today.

2. What physical movements or experience(s) could you incorporate into your classroom or lesson planning that would help support your students?

Chapter 20

Trauma Separates Us, a Summary

"Relationships matter: the currency for systemic change was trust, and trust comes through forming healthy working relationships. People, not programs, change people." ~ Bruce D. Perry

Every person is wired for the need to connect with other human beings. We cannot survive on our own. And, by forming strong bonds we can increase our chances of survival dramatically. This is why babies form close bonds with their parents almost instantly after birth. We are also wired to seek out safety. Our bodies will do whatever is necessary to achieve a feeling of safety. But, what happens when our need for connection is placed against our need for safety?

Unfortunately, this unwinnable equation is what some of your students live with everyday. They desperately want to connect with other people, to meet their primary need for connections. Unfortunately, the vast majority of trauma that your students are suffering from is interpersonal. That means that the majority of your students were hurt by other people. Their brains quickly wired themselves to view other people as a threat, and many students will distance themselves from human contact because they are unconsciously trying to achieve safety. These students will push teachers and peers away because their brain views these people as potential threats, but this leaves the student's need for connection unmet. All of us have seen students cycle back and forth between trying to socialize and isolating. This is their attempt to meet both of these basic needs of connection and safety. We know from research that close, loving, healthy relationships will help our traumatized students heal. How do we provide this when their brains are wired for safety? Here's a summary of so much of what we've discussed:

1) Recognize when your students are in the back of the brain and try not to take those behaviors personally. When a student is triggered they will push you alway with their behavior or self-isolate. While frustrating to you as an educator, this is normal. This is a coping strategy designed to keep them safe. Recognize the behavior for what it is and focus your energy on helping the student cope so that they can return to the front of the brain.

2) Teach them relationship skills. Many of our students aren't growing up in homes where family members calmly explain their side of the situation and come to healthy compromises. Some of your students have only seen adults deal with conflict with yelling or violence. They lack the conflict resolution skills necessary to make any relationship last because they lack the skills necessary to deal with conflict in a healthy way.

All relationships have conflict but how we deal with this conflict determines the quality of our relationships. I spend a lot of time with students to help them learn how to deal with conflict at home and with peers, helping them to understand the other person's perspective and guiding them to reduce the conflict in healthy ways. Most importantly, if no one ever takes the time to teach these skills, how will they ever acquire them? In all likelihood, they might not and then be more likely to pass down unhealthy coping skills to their children.

3) Be kind everyday. Every time you interact with students you are wiring them to the front or the back of the brain. I take this very seriously. I

know these interactions add up quickly. I also know that my most challenging students are the ones who need my kindness the most. Your words matter. How you make your students feel matters. They might remember your kind words the rest of their lives. It's that important. I don't think enough teachers realize that their smiles are a superpower. Every teacher in the world can impact their students in a profound way by smiling. A smile could literally save a life. I challenge you to smile at every student who walks into your classroom. Imagine if a student has seven different teachers tell them that they are excited to see them and greet them with a big smile everyday. Imagine if every educator consistently practiced the 10:1 positive interaction ratio. Can you imagine the impact that would have on that student by the end of the quarter, let alone after thirteen years of education?

4) Get them plugged in. The more positive people a student has in their life the quicker they will recover from trauma and thrive. We want these students plugged into everything, sports, band, clubs, Big Brother/Big Sisters, etc. Every mentor who enters their life could end up being the person who changes their life. I know as a football coach I want every

kid in the building involved with my program, because in my opinion high school football is the best at-risk program in the country. I want the challenging kids in my program because I know they will be around great men of character who will love and mentor them. Some of these students are very challenging and might not be eligible for games, but if we are only supporting the students that are doing well then we are failing our purpose as a program.

Hero Spotlight: Kerri Ferrai

Kerri is a Director of Alternative Education. She is incredible at rallying her community around the students she serves. Kerri increased the graduation rate of the local alternative school by 540% in two years. Her school district had the highest graduation rates in over a decade. How did she do it? She started by understanding that she needed to meet the needs of the whole child. She took the time to build amazing relationships and to identify the barriers that were preventing her students from being successful. Next, she created amazing community partnerships. She partnered with faith-based organizations to provide her students with cooking and budget classes. She also partnered with Tru Manufacturing and they mentored her students, provided tours of the facility, and even gave Thanksgiving and Christmans celebrations. Many of her students went on to have careers with this organization.

5) Lastly, let them know you care and they are not alone. You will not be able to fix the vast majority of your students' problems. But, the trauma they are experiencing isn't the problem, being ALONE with the trauma is the problem. It's heartbreaking to hear their stories and know you can not change their situation. But, you can listen and assure them that they will not go through this alone. I tell my students all the time that "this sucks", but they are not alone. I'm going to be there with them through it. This can be a life saving conversation. These students feel alone and they cannot imagine a better life but you can let them know you care and you'll help them through this difficult season of life.

Reflection Questions

1. How can we make sure our students don't feel alone with their problems?

2. How can we make sure every student feels connected to at least one adult in our building?

3. What concept from this book sticks with you the most or has changed how you think about how you teach and/or care for your students?

Chapter 21

Ideological Warning & Teacher Self-Care

"Almost everything will work again if you unplug it for a few minutes, including you." ~ Anne Lamott

Meeting our most challenging students with love and acceptance is unfortunately a revolutionary and radical concept to most of the country. For decades we've met these traumatized students with harsh punishments and expulsions. When you start down this trauma-informed care path, it's important to understand you will be met with resistance. Not everyone is ready for this significant change and many people will push back against your efforts. School administrators might receive resistance from teachers and parents. Teachers might feel push back from administrators. I want you to know that this is normal. Anytime you are blazing a new trail, people who are invested in the old way can feel threatened. I've dealt with this several times during my career and seen other pioneers face the same resistance in their schools and communities.

As an example, as a community-based mental health professional, I found out that one of our psychiatrists was a heavy prescriber, accepting tens of thousands of dollars from pharmaceutical companies for "speaking fees." I brought this information to my director because I felt that it was a huge conflict of interest that he prescribed these medications frequently for the children I worked with and now he was getting large payments from these drug companies. I was told that the behavior was unethical but not illegal so he would be allowed to continue. I quickly found out after this that I began to be treated with hostility by one of the organization's top administrators despite years of perfect performance reviews. It worked against me to speak against the accepted system.

As a teacher I've spoken with administrators about how their frequent use of suspension and expulsion lead to high dropout rates and how using restorative practices can keep these students in our community and help them learn at the same time. For some, instead of being encouraged by thinking about the needs of our most vulnerable students, I was reprimanded.

I write about all this to remind you that advocating for the most vulnerable people in your community can be dangerous work. You might be met with resistance, you may feel alone at times, but the work is too important to ignore.

Teacher Self-Care

Education is a hard profession, often made even harder by the important work of educating traumatized students. It's essential that all educators have a self-care plan they follow. Our work is emotionally depleting and if we're not continually investing ourselves we'll quickly be worn down, thus becoming less effective with our students. I've taught hundreds of educators how to make a simple yet effective self-care plans. It's incredible how these easy to implement strategies can have a huge impact on your life when you consistently follow them.

Just like with our students, every person's self-care plan is going to look different. It's a very personal journey to figure out what replenishes our souls. Below, I break self-care into five categories. Don't worry if one category isn't as appealing to you as the others. They don't have to be split equally five ways. Some people spend way more time with physical self-care while others are more into their spirituality. Remember every plan is different. Focus on what sounds appealing to you.

1) **Sensory:** Sensory self-care is all about learning to calm your mind. The more you engage in your senses the more you'll be in the present moment. Our worries about the past and future melt away when we are truly engaged in our senses: Sight, taste, touch, smell, and hearing. Examples of sensory self-care include:

    - Looking into a fire
    - Smelling the fresh air outdoors
    - Cuddling a soft blanket
    - Feeling the warm sensation on your skin in a bath or shower
    - Feeling your breath
    - Listening to music
    - Feeling the warm sun on your skin
    - Enjoying a small piece of chocolate
    - Walking barefoot in the grass

- Essential oils
- Enjoying a cup of coffee
- A massage
- Listening to the sounds in nature
- Petting your dog or cat

2) **Emotional:** Emotional self care is about fully engaging your emotions and fully expressing what you are feeling. Too often we push down the feelings we don't enjoy like anger and sadness. Learning to express our emotions fully is essential to being a healthy person. Remember, there are no good or bad emotions, they are all just information. All emotions need to be fully expressed in a healthy way and giving yourself an opportunity to express them will help you feel better. I tell my students, "A pain shared is a pain halved." We all need someone in our lives with whom we can share our painful moments. This is how we heal. Examples of emotional self-care include:

- Journaling your feelings about your day
- Seeing a therapist (most educators have a limited number of free sessions through your EAP program)

- Expanding your emotional vocabulary by writing down feeling words or using a "feeling wheel"
- Make time for people who truly "get you." Have weekly check in with those important people.
- Fully express what you're feeling. Men, it's ok to be sad. We need to get better at expressing our sadness.
- Engage in activities that make you laugh. I watch Chris Farely Youtube videos during my plan period.
- Listen to music that expresses what feelings you're currently experiencing.

3) **Spiritual:** Spiritual self-care isn't just about believing in God. It's about getting in touch with your values and what's important to you. People who are struggling with depression typically respond better when they're able to tap into a larger purpose. Examples of spiritual self-care include:

- Daily prayer, meditation, or mindfulness
- Attending a religious service
- Reading poetry

- Walking in nature and being mindful of all the beauty
- Make a gratitude list everyday of ten things you are thankful for
- Be creative: paint, draw, write, dance, music, photography
- Make a list of five things that make you feel alive and incorporate those things into your week
- Say positive affirmations daily
- Go on a trip

4) **Physical:** Physical self-care isn't just about keeping your body healthy. It's also great for blowing off steam. Physical self-care is all about movement. The biggest mistake I see people make is thinking that this has to be a grind. If you hate doing it, it won't become a habit. Find exercises you enjoy and it will be much more likely to become part of your routine. Getting proper sleep and nutrition are also important. Examples of physical self-care include:

- Dance
- Yoga. Don't be intimidated, they have classes for beginners and the benefits are incredible.
- Joining a class or rec team

- Running or walking with your dog
- Go for a walk
- Nature hikes
- Swimming
- Exercise videos online
- Biking
- Lifting weights

5) **Social:** Social self-care is going to look different for every person. Some people have dozens of friends they constantly are engaged with, while others choose to have a handful or close relationships and/or need their alone time. Social self-care is all about spending time with people who empower you and you feel better after spending time with them. Examples of social self-care include:
    - Go on a lunch or dinner date with someone you value
    - Video chat with someone who you care about but lives far away
    - Reach out to someone who you haven't spoken to in a while

- Join a group of people who have the same interest as you. For example I'm part of a mid Missouri Pearl Jam club.
- Stop spending time with people who deplete or disempower you
- Join a support group
- Sign up for a class, learn a new skill, and meet people at the same time.

Again, remember everyone's plan is going to look different. You may spend more of your free time on social self-care and your friend might be all about emotional self-care. That's ok, everyone's plan will look different. This is what my self-care plan looks like:

- Social: I have a group call with my college roommates every Sunday.
- Emotional: I share my feelings with my wife and I've been to therapy.
- Physical: I love hiking and walking after work while listening to music.
- Sensory: I enjoy nature walks and really engage all my senses.

- Spiritual: I go to church every Sunday.

I encourage you to build your own plan and commit to it. You'll be amazed at how much these little things can increase your life satisfaction.

Reflection Questions

1. What resistance can you anticipate as you begin to advocate and/or operate in a more trauma-informed way as an educator?

2. Build your own stress management plan. Share it with someone close to you. Post it somewhere you will see it everyday.

Chapter 22

Johnny's Story…Continued

"Trauma is a fact of life. It does not, however, have to be a life sentence. Not only can trauma be healed, but with appropriate guidance and support, it can be transformative." ~ Peter A. Levine

I'm excited to report that Johnny is a middle schooler now and he's doing well. He's doing well academically, has lots of friends, and has great relationships at home. I remember learning as a graduate student that early childhood trauma was the most challenging to heal from, so how is this possible? Johnny is a success story because he had several heroes in his life. He had a grandmother who dropped all of her life plans to raise her grandson. He had a kindergarten teacher who loved him everyday despite his challenging behaviors. He had a school counselor who literally took a punch in the face for him, who loved him and supported him through his darkest days. He had a hero principal who chose to keep loving and supporting him when so many others would have taken the easy path and sent him away. It took a lot of heroes to change his life.

As we conclude…

Who are the Johnnys in your school?

And, do you believe this could happen for them?

My deepest thanks and gratitude to each of you all for the work you do.

Acknowledgements

Writing this book was more challenging and overwhelming than I could have imagined. This book would never have happened without my friend Anne Rulo. She helped walk me through this process, kept me motivated and gave me the confidence to release it. I'm forever grateful for her guidance and wisdom throughout this process.

I'm grateful for Michelle Oliver. She encouraged me to write this book and helped me form it in its infancy. Without her support I never would have moved this book past the idea stage.

Thank you Victor Bell for encouraging me in my trauma-informed work. Early on I lacked the confidence to share this message and he continually encouraged me to grow. He saw something in me that I never saw in myself until years later.

Thank you to my family for your lifelong support. My father fostered my work ethic. My mother taught me unconditional love. My brother Jeremy and sisters Melissa and Miranda have been tremendous lifelong supports. My beautiful children Justina, Claire, and Hayden have been the greatest blessings of my life. Watching them grow up into wonderful people is one of the greatest joys of my life.

Thank you to my wife Ashley. You have been my biggest supporter. You help me grow everyday. Without you none of this would be possible. Thank you for wisdom, strength and love.

Resources & References

Apps, Books, Podcasts, & Websites

- **Apps:** Headspace and Calm are good apps to help with you and your students mental health. These apps can help you sleep, meditate, or just relax. I really enjoy the sound of rain on a window when I sleep from my Calm app. The app, "Anxiety Release with Bilateral Stimulation" is a quality app that helps with anxiety. It has a small fee.

- **Books:**

    The Body Keeps Score by Dr Bessel Van Der Kolk

    The Boy Who was Raised As A Dog by Dr. Bruce Perry

    What Happened to You by Dr. Bruce Perry & Oprah Winfrey

    Waking the Tiger: Healing Trauma by Peter A. Levine

    In the Realm of Hungry Ghosts by Dr. Gabor Mate

    The Deepest Well by Nadine Burke Harris

    Hacking School Discipline by Nathan Maynard and Brad Weinstein

- **Podcasts:**

    The Trauma Educators Network Podcast

    The Therapist Uncensored

    The Brian Mendler Show PodCast

    Polyvagal Podcast

References

Goodman, R. D., Miller, M. D., & West-Olatunji, C. A. (2012). Traumatic stress, socioeconomic status, and academic achievement among primary school students. *Psychological Trauma: Theory, Research, Practice, and Policy,* 4(3), 252–259. https://doi.org/10.1037/a0024912

Delaney-Black V., Covington C., Ondersma S. J., Nordstrom-Klee B., Templin T., Ager J., Sokol R. (2002). Violence exposure, trauma, and IQ and/or reading deficits among urban children. *Archives of Pediatrics & Adolescent Medicine,* 156, 280–285. https://doi.org/10.1001/archpedi.156.3.280

Webster, E. M. (2022). The Impact of Adverse Childhood Experiences on Health and Development in Young Children. Global Pediatric Health, 9, 2333794X2210787. https://doi.org/10.1177/2333794x221078708

Wolopow, R., Johnson, M. M., Hertel, R., & Kinkaid, S.O. (2009). *The heart of learning and teaching compassion, resiliency, and academic Success.* https://www.ksdetasn.org/resources/1503

Made in the USA
Middletown, DE
22 March 2025